AF427888

England: Cultured, Charming, and Classic

A Guide to Hidden England
The Hidden Gems Series

Christy Nicholas

Green Dragon Publishing

2026 Edition

Published by Green Dragon Publishing
Beacon Falls, CT
www.GreenDragonArtist.com
All rights reserved.

TABLE OF CONTENTS

INTRODUCTION

What images come to mind when you think of England? Do you imagine Sherlock Holmes stalking the back alleys of Victorian London? Or the windswept moors of Yorkshire, covered in heather? Or perhaps the dramatic coastline and chalky white cliffs of Dover?

But what lies beyond the trappings of red telephone boxes, Roman baths, and bittersweet Dickensian tales? What is the authentic England, the very essence of the country that remains alluring and steadfast?

This is not simply about tea served in dainty china, cricket matches on village greens, or the iconic chimes of Big Ben. It's the unseen spirit of the land, the richly woven tapestry of history and tradition that ceaselessly beckons the wanderlust-filled hearts.

Every person will hold a different vision of England in their mind, whether they've visited or not. It might be a video of a royal wedding, a much-loved show on PBS or BBC America, or a classic novel like Pride and Prejudice. The food, landscape, history, music, or a combination of all of these can speak to the heart.

There is a wealth of fascinating things to do, stunning places to see, and friendly people to meet in London, the Cotswolds, or in the North. Be it the shifting landscape of rolling hills in the Lake District, or the seaside town carnivals, these aspects change with your perspective, and with time, to reveal previously hidden depths.

I have always had a special fondness for England and English history. My mother lived in England for a few years before I was born, and a good chunk of my ancestry comes from that country.

I first visited in 1996 as part of a week-long trip to Somerset with a group of new age hippies. Well, the part with the hippies was a week, but I went over for two weeks. Four days in Ireland, three days in London, and then I went to Somerset.

My three days in London were eye-opening as this was my first trip overseas (that I was old enough to remember, at least). I took the touristy hop-on/hop-off tour around the city, experienced the hordes of people, rode the Underground, ate fish & chips, and wandered around Piccadilly Circus and Hyde Park.

The hippie new age group visited some of the classic magical sites, such as Avebury Stone Circle, Bath, West Kennet Longbarrow, and Wookey Hole. It was a delightful introduction to the rural part of England.

I've been back several times, exploring different parts of the country, and I always feel welcome and centered in England.

In this book, I will explore many aspects of England. I will delve into the history and myths that shaped the culture, as well as the superstitions and beliefs that still hold sway today.

Parts of that are, of course, the religious traditions, the deep and varied history, and the various invasions from European cultures.

I shall talk about the food, the music, the people, and, of course, the drinks. Some practical aspects to planning your trip, and your photography, are next, as well as some discounts and tricks to save some money. And, of course, a nice big section on hidden gems, places off the beaten track, to get away from the busloads of tourists and find your own special places.

Please, enjoy your journey through my book. And, if I have convinced you to travel to this incredible place, please let me know. I think everyone should visit England and be enriched by this incredibly cultured, charming, and classic land.

HISTORY AND MYTH
What We Know and What We Believe

Prehistoric (to 55 BCE)

In the hushed whispers of antiquity, England was not the proud and solitary island we know today. She stood as a majestic peninsula, her verdant expanses reaching out from the heart of Europe, her feet caressed by the capricious sea.

As a stalwart outpost, she watched the world. Her form was cradled by the vast, unruly ocean, waiting for the tides of time to sculpt her into the insular queen she would become.

The oldest remains we have discovered so far belong to a previous species of human, *Homo heidelbergensis*, who lived in

England around 500,000 years ago. Since then, Neanderthals visited the island and then modern humans.

The earliest known cave art dates from about 13,000 years ago, in the Creswell Crags in Derbyshire. This was near the end of the last Ice Age, and as the ice faded away, people seeped into the land now known as England. These were nomadic hunters, living off the land before the advent of farming.

Come with me, back to a time when wooly mammoths still roamed the earth, and England was but a twinkle in the eye of history. When Neolithic hunters crossed a land bridge from the European mainland around 6,500 BCE, they found an island covered with forests and teeming with wildlife.

Then, in a torrential flood, the sea ate the land bridge between England and the continent, separating the island forever more.

When agriculture arrived in England around 4,000 BCE, they farmed pulses, wheat, and barley. They were still nomadic, but they usually had trackways and common areas. They built communal monuments, like Windmill Hill or West Kennet Long Barrow in Wiltshire.

Imagine living in this time. Moving to a new area each season, constructing temporary houses of wattle-and-daub with conical thatched roofs, hunting deer or fishing for food, gathering in groups at the solstice celebrations.

This is also the time when stone circles and megalithic structures dominated the land, such as Castlerigg, Silbury Hill, Avebury, and the most famous of them all, Stonehenge. There are hundreds of these monuments around the country, some no more than ankle-high remnants of once proud and tall stones.

As the Bronze Age arrived around 2,300 BCE, the natives, who we call the Beaker People, started settling down a little more. They started burying their dead in elaborate graves, rather than cremating them.

They discovered the tin mines in Cornwall and learned how to make bronze for weapons and tools. They traded with other areas in a complex network. The first hillforts were built, such as Old Sarum in Wiltshire. Yes, Wiltshire was home to a great many ancient sites.

Then, the Iron Age technology arrived in England, and the hillforts grew massive, like Maiden Castle in Dorset, or Old Oswestry in Shropshire.

With iron tools came better weapons, and with better weapons came better warriors. A hierarchy built around fighting prowess grew prevalent, and small family units morphed into larger tribal groups.

Roman Era (55 BCE—410 CE)

The Romans first arrived in Britain in 55-54 BCE, and their occupation as Romans lasted until at least 410 CE. During that time, they conducted a few invasions, starting with Julius Caesar, Agricola, and Aulus Plautius.

Once the Romans established a foothold in the south, they shifted to a policy of setting up trading agreements with certain tribal chiefs of the Celtic tribes. There were a series of rebellions led by Caracticus and Boudicca.

Boudicca was a queen of the Icenii tribe, and when the Roman soldiers flogged and violated her daughters, she led an incredibly successful series of raids. She destroyed several colonies, including Camulodunum (Colchester) and London.

Another initiative of the Romans was to conquer and destroy the Druids, the priest caste of the ancient natives of Britain. The Romans raided the Druids' traditional center at Anglesey, known as Mona.

There is a fascinating book by Bryan Sykes, called *Saxons, Vikings, and Celts: The Genetic Roots of Britain and Ireland*. The book explores the DNA evidence of settlement and invasion by the various groups into England, Ireland, England, and Wales, and comes to some fascinating conclusions about these invasions.

Early Middle Ages (410 CE—1066 CE)

This time used to be known as the Dark Ages, a time of murky tales, lofty legends, and transformative turmoil. However, the more recent name of Early Medieval Age is more descriptive, and less dramatic.

As the Roman legions receded, invaders emerged from the mysterious mists of the North Sea, the Angles, Saxons, and Jutes.

Wielding axe and shield, they descended upon Britain, pushing the indigenous Celtic Britons westward into what's now Wales and Cornwall.

Old Sarum, Salisbury

These years were a tumultuous mosaic of tribal rivalries, petty kingdoms, and heroic warriors. Legends of King Arthur and the saga of Beowulf stirred the hearts of the people, echoing in the mead halls amidst the clatter of ale-horns and the thrum of lyres. Within this chaotic tapestry, England, or "Angle-land," began to form.

In 597 CE, Pope Gregory I sent Augustine to convert the residents of this island to Christianity. He set up his archbishopric in

Canterbury, a place that still holds ecclesiastical prominence today. The monks, with their skills in literacy and organization, were the glue binding society together, and their monasteries, beacons of learning and artistry, dotted the landscape, at least until Henry VIII came along.

Skilled Anglo-Saxon artisans crafted intricate jewelry, like the mesmerizing gold and garnet pieces found at Sutton Hoo. The beauty of the illuminated manuscripts, such as the Lindisfarne Gospels, is a timeless treasure.

Then, from the icy fjords of the North, Viking dragon-ships appeared. These seaborne raiders, drawn by wealth and opportunity, attacked Lindisfarne, the first in an endless series of raids. Monasteries burned, and kingdoms fell, but the Viking Age was not merely one of destruction. They founded vibrant cities, introduced new technologies, and spurred England into becoming a more unified entity under one of the era's greatest figures, Alfred the Great.

Taking the throne of Wessex in 871 CE, Alfred battled valiantly against the invaders. A lover of learning, he also invited scholars to his court and initiated the Anglo-Saxon Chronicle, providing a priceless historical resource, one of the few written sources historians now have of those years.

Following Alfred, the threads of the English tapestry began to weave tighter. His dynasty reclaimed lands from the Vikings, culminating in Æthelstan's reign.

But Sweyn Forkbeard, a Danish king, and his son Cnut, cast a new wave of Viking dominance over the island. Cnut, ruling an empire spanning England, Denmark, and Norway, fostered a period of prosperity.

The Early Medieval Age ended in 1066 CE with the Battle of Hastings, the last successful invasion of England. The victorious Norman Duke, William the Conqueror, ushered in the era of medieval kings and castles.

So, the Early Medieval Age of England, a time shrouded in obscurity, was, in fact, a crucible in which the country was forged. A chaotic yet captivating period, bristling with raw human spirit, epic sagas, resolute resistance, and the dawn of a nation that would stride forth into the annals of history.

Medieval Period (1066 CE—1485 CE)

The saga begins with the Battle of Hastings in 1066 CE, when William the Conqueror seized the English crown, based on a promise he was given by Edward the Confessor. His reign introduced a pantheon of castles and cathedrals, and a huge influx of French terms into the budding English language.

In the 12th century, the struggle for the crown between Stephen I and the Empress Maud tore the country into bits. The resulting chaos, termed The Anarchy, resulted in a widespread breakdown in law and order. This conflict set the stage for the later War of the Roses.

In 1215, King John signed the Magna Carta, an iconic parchment that limited royal power and set the stage for governance drama. It was the seed from which the great tree of parliamentary democracy would grow.

Life wasn't all chivalry and cathedrals, though. The Black Death, an uninvited guest in the 14th century, left devastation in its wake. Yet, even this tragedy wove a strange silver lining, weakening the feudal system and stirring up societal change. This resulted in the eventual end of the serf class with the reign of Elizabeth I.

The Middle Ages also shone with the luster of courtly love and heroic knights. Tales of King Arthur and the knights of his round table whispered of honor and bravery, and Richard the Lionheart's exploits stirred the heartstrings of his homeland.

This era nurtured minds and sowed the seeds of scholarly pursuit with the foundation of great centers of learning at Oxford and Cambridge. It cultivated the arts, with Geoffrey Chaucer's Canterbury Tales painting a vibrant tapestry of medieval life and mystery lighting the spark of English drama.

And it fostered the growing English Language as William Caxton printed a Bible in the vernacular.

Between 1337 and 1453 CE, the Hundred Years War with France saw the pendulum of fortune swing back and forth, and the Wars of the Roses turned England's nobility into a garden of thorns, each fighting for the crown.

The curtain closed upon the Middle Ages at the Battle of Bosworth in 1485. With his victory, Henry Tudor (the Earl of Richmond) ascended the throne as Henry VII, heralding the era of the Tudors and the dawn of the Renaissance.

The medieval period of England was indeed a vibrant maelstrom of progress and paradox. This era, like an ancient storyteller, continues to whisper its tales in the shadow of castle ruins, the silence of old cathedrals, and the pages of immortal literature.

The Renaissance Era (early 16th century to early 17th century)

The curtain rose in 1485 with the end of the Wars of the Roses at the Battle of Bosworth. A new dynasty, the Tudors, ascended the throne, personified by Henry VII, a shrewd consolidator of power. His son, Henry VIII, remembered for his six wives and even more significant religious shakeup, broke with the Pope and established the Church of England, changing the country's spiritual and political landscape.

Next on the throne was Elizabeth I, the "Virgin Queen," who navigated her reign with political savvy. This period was an

English Renaissance, a time of blossoming arts, epitomized by the works of Shakespeare, Spencer, and Arthur Broke. It was a time of exploration, with figures like Sir Francis Drake taking to the seas. Her reign was also fraught with tension, as the threat from Catholic Spain culminated in the defeat of the Spanish Armada.

Enter the Stuarts. The era started with James I, the first king of both England and Scotland combined. His reign was marked by the famous "Gunpowder Plot," an unsuccessful attempt by Guy Fawkes to blow up the king and Parliament.

But the defining feature of this era was a rising conflict between the monarchy and Parliament, which erupted into the Civil War under Charles I. The King's execution sent shockwaves through the realm.

Oliver Cromwell, leading the Commonwealth, filled the void, but the republic was transitory. After Cromwell's death, the monarchy was restored under Charles II, the "Merry Monarch," whose reign saw the rebirth of arts and sciences but also the plague and the Great Fire of London.

The Glorious Revolution in 1688 marked a decisive shift in England's governance. When James II's Catholicism rankled, William of Orange, his Protestant son-in-law, was invited to seize the throne. A law was passed making it illegal for a member of the royal family to be Catholic. William and Mary ruled as co-monarchs, but the monarchy's power began to wane against the rising strength of Parliament.

English colonies took root in the New World, and trade expanded, bringing wealth but also triggering the dark legacy of the transatlantic slave trade.

The period ended in 1714 with the death of Queen Anne, the last Stuart monarch. A new dynasty, the Hanoverians, began their reign with George I, setting the stage for an age of empire. Neither Anne nor any of the kings through George III spoke English.

From 1485 to 1714, England transformed dramatically. It was a saga of religious revolution, political transformation, cultural flourishing, and colonial expansion. This period, poised between the medieval and the modern, shaped the English identity and planted the seeds that would grow into the world's largest empire.

Enlightenment and Industrial Revolution (18th to 19th century)

The 18th century saw the flowering of the Enlightenment, with England leading in philosophy, science, and political thought. The Industrial Revolution started, transforming English society from agrarian to industrial, from rural to urban. While this brought significant social and economic upheaval, it laid the groundwork for modern society.

The Georgian era was followed by the Victorian age, marked by Queen Victoria's long reign, vast expansion of the British Empire, and cultural developments in literature, arts, and science. Authors like Charles Dickens commented on the era's social problems, while engineers like Isambard Kingdom Brunel built railways and steamships.

20th Century to 21st Century

As the Victorian Era came to an end, World War I and II profoundly affected the nation, leading to massive loss and reshaping its global role. The post-war period saw the establishment of the welfare state, including the National Health Service.

The latter half of the century brought decolonization, resulting in a multi-ethnic society. The 60s were "swinging," a result of the new prosperity after a long time of rationing after World War II. They listened to the Beatles and the Rolling Stones. This new generation created a cultural revolution and a British Invasion of music into America.

More recently, Britain faced significant challenges, such as economic recession and the controversial Brexit.

There's still so much to tell about England's captivating history, filled with resilience, invention, passion, and constant transformation. A story that continually unfolds, each day adding a new word, sentence, or chapter to its rich and complex narrative.

SUPERSTITIONS AND BELIEFS

The world of myth is filled with fairies, creatures of mystery, curses, blessings, hidden treasure, and dark souls in the night. Every realm of creativity touches on these subjects. Literature, film, music, art, dance all delight the mind and the imagination with sprites, goblins, and pixies.

England's traditions are certainly no exception.

Some of the tales and beliefs in the English countryside are shared by other groups of Celts, such as the fairies, others are unique to the English pantheon of beliefs. While Ireland has a more cohesive set of these "fairy tales," there are several that were shared with England, Wales, and England, and many that could be leftovers from the Briton times.

I find English myths have a lighter flavor than most of the Irish myths do. Perhaps this is because the country itself is a bit gentler in its mountains and coastlines.

But these tales could still chill the heart when told around a fire in the dark night. The audience wouldn't be idle while the stories were told. Listeners could be spinning, or mending a harness, or whittling buttons, but they listened as the stories were told.

Do keep in mind that the English fairy beliefs, as well as modern pagan beliefs, are a living tradition. Please treat them with respect.

The Tower of London Ravens

Charles II was told that if ravens were ever to leave the Tower of London, that the White Tower would fall, and a great disaster would befall the kingdom. Therefore, Charles II decreed that a group of ravens should be kept in the Tower at all times, their wings clipped to keep them close.

Fairies

While most of the fairy folklore we think of today came from the Celtic tales of Ireland and England, some aspects of those legends have made their way into English folklore.

These were the original pre-Christian divinities of Gaelic England. The takeover of Christianity reduced these beings to hold only diminutive powers, also known as the *Tuatha dè Danaan* in Irish folklore.

Fairies often guard particular places, such as a hill, a hawthorn tree, a loch or wood. Dusk and dawn are particularly dangerous to encounter them, as are the feasts of Samhain, Bealtaine, and Midsummer (summer solstice).

Most of the English use of fairies is in literature like medieval romances, Edmund Spenser and The Faerie Queene, Shakespeare's Midsummer Night's Dream, and to the modern era with J. R. R. Tolkien's Middle-Earth saga.

Arthurian Legends

While there may be some historic basis for the tales, most scholars agree that King Arthur's tales are mostly fabricated or a conflation of several leaders who lived in the Early Medieval Age.

The legendary Arthur is familiar to most people as the king who made England safe from raiding Anglo-Saxons and formed the Knights of the Round Table. These knights went on various quests, especially for the Holy Grail. He had a mystical sword, Excalibur, gifted to him by the Lady of the Lake, and his main advisor was the equally legendary wizard, Merlin.

Spring-Heeled Jack

This legend dates to Victorian times, a terrifying man with the ability to make stupendous leaps. His hands were claws and his eyes were red balls of fire. Some said he wore a helmet and a white oilskin garment.

The Legend of the Lambton Worm

John Lambton, the heir to the Lambton Estate, was rumored to have battled a giant worm or dragon that was terrorizing the local town.

John only managed to defeat this creature by preparing his armor as per a witch's instructions, with spearheads all over it. When the worm tries to crush him, it cuts itself to pieces.

However, there was a curse. John must kill the first creature he sees after killing the worm. Even though he was warned, his father rushes to congratulate John. Even though he tries to thwart the curse by killing his favorite dog instead, the family is cursed for nine generations.

Hairy Hands of Dartmoor, Devon

Related to the *bean sì* of Irish legend, this spirit attaches itself to a family or clan and keens with the mourning of an upcoming death.

The White Wizard and the White Mare, Alderly Edge

A farmer from Mobberly was going to sell his mare at market. He met an old man dressed in white, who offered to buy it, but the farmer thought he could get a better price in town.

However, he had no luck and returned to the old man, who led him into a secret place, with ancient knights sleeping on the ground. These knights were to wake and fight in the hour of the country's greatest need.

The farmer was paid with gold coins and led outside, and the secret entrance shut, never to be seen again.

John O' Kent, Hertfordshire

Possibly from around the 13th century, John o' Kent or John of Kent was an old hermit with supernatural powers. There are tales of him outwitting the devil or selling his soul to the devil to have supernatural power.

Sometimes he uses these powers for good, such as building a bridge in a single night. However, the Devil could have the soul of the first to cross. Jack sent a starving dog over the bridge, and the Devil took what he could get.

There are some who believe that John O'Kent wrote A Midsummer Night's Dream, rather than Shakespeare.

The Fairy Hills of Cumbria

There are a few fairy sites in this area.

Elva Hill on the banks of Bassenthwaite Lake. The hill is said to hide a gateway to the Otherworld, which only opens at certain times of the year. There is a Neolithic stone circle which originally had about thirty standing stones, but only half remain.

King Eveling's Rath is in the old Roman Fort of Mediobogdum. Tradition claims that a fairy rath stands within the site, and it's possible the name is derived from the Old Norse word for Elf. It also holds associations with King Arthur legends.

Another place related to King Arthur is the Castle Rock of Triermain. It looks like an ancient castle, and supposedly King Arthur and a host of fairies visited, while Gwendolyn was sent into an enchanted sleep by Merlin.

Dick Whittington

Richard Whittington was a real person who lived in the late 14th/early 15th century. He was a wealthy merchant and Lord Mayor of London. However, many stories tell of his rise from an impoverished youth and prophecies of his rise to power. This tale is a favorite in British pantomimes.

Beast of Bodmin Moor

The creature is panther-like, and black furred, and it stalks around Bodmin Moor in Cornwall, England, killing livestock. It's supposedly a phantom, because big cats shouldn't be in England's moors. This is a modern legend, dating from the 20ᵗʰ century.

Sir Gawain and the Green Knight

Part of the Arthurian legends, this tale is one of the more popular, and has recently been made into a movie. The tale itself dates from the late 14ᵗʰ century and describes a game where each opponent is to behead the other to win. It draws on many sources, such as Welsh, Irish, and English stories.

Sir Gawain accepts a challenge from a mysterious visitor, a knight who is all green (or dressed in green). The dare is that whoever strikes him will be struck in return, in a year and a day.

The Lincoln Imp

There is a grotesque sculpture in the Lincoln Cathedral which, according to a 14ᵗʰ century tale, is rumored to be a creature sent by Satan, but turned into stone by an angel who emerged from a book of hymns.

Robin Hood

The tales of Robin Hood vie with King Arthur as the most popular English tale. It's widely debated if he was ever a true person, though he may be based on several people, or even be a title held by many.

In the legend, he was an excellent archer and a nobleman turned outlaw who gathered a group of Merry Men in Sherwood Forest, near Nottingham. This group targeted rich travelers, stole their coins and jewels, and distributed the stolen wealth to the poor.

The first tales of Robin Hood, however, have no mention of the common characters in the tales today, such as Maid Marian or Friar Tuck. The Sheriff of Nottingham is the clear antagonist, and Robin is joined by Little John, Will Scarlet, and Much the Miller's Son.

Stonehenge

Stonehenge, located in Wiltshire, England, is one of the world's most famous prehistoric monuments. Built in several stages from approximately 3,000 BCE to 1,600 BCE, it features a unique, circular arrangement of standing stones, some weighing up to 25 tons. Its construction and purpose have puzzled scholars for centuries, but it is thought to have served as a ceremonial or religious site.

It's aligned with the movements of the sun, suggesting a possible astronomical function. Some stones were sourced from over 150 miles away, a remarkable achievement for the Neolithic people.

Despite modern archeological studies, many mysteries of Stonehenge remain unsolved, contributing to its enduring allure. It's a UNESCO World Heritage Site and an iconic symbol of Britain's ancient past.

St. George and the Dragon

The story of Saint George, or at least that type of story, has ancient origins. Jason and Medea, Perseus and Andromeda, there is always a hero fighting a fearsome monster to save an innocent woman from being a sacrifice.

Even after Christianization, the legend wore several other faces first, such as St. Theodore or St. Demetrius.

But St. George is not only an integral legend to England; he's the patron saint. The legend says that he went to save the princess, but he offered to kill the dragon if the city promised to become Christian.

The Holy Grail

Though I touched on this with the discussion of King Arthur, I think the Holy Grail deserves its own section. Legend has it that the grail was carried to Britain by Joseph of Arimathea. He came to what is now Glastonbury and planted a tree there, which still grows to this day.

There is much debate about the shape of the grail. It might be a wooden bowl, a gold salver, a jeweled chalice, or, if Dan Brown is to be believed, the child of Christ.

Changelings

Sickly offspring of Fairies who are secretly switched in place of a human child. If you can see them with True Sight, they appear as little old men or women. The human child usually dies shortly afterwards.

London Eye

The Green Man

According to some sources, ancient pagan traditions speak of the Green Man, a symbol of rebirth and the cycle of seasons. He is usually portrayed with a face of branches or vines, leaves or flowers.

There are many architectural images of him through both churches and secular buildings, especially in Gothic architecture.

The foliate face of the Green Man may be a descendent of Bacchus or Dionysus, gods of wine and revelry. There is also a Christian connection to the Quest of Seth; the twigs and seeds planted under Adam's tongue by his son, Seth.

The Green Children of Woolpit

Around the 12th century, stories of two children mysteriously appearing in Woolpit started. Not only did they appear from nowhere, they had green skin and couldn't speak the local language.

While they were adopted by Sir Richard de Calne, fed, and clothed, learning English, and finally explained their origin as the "land of St. Martin." But no one knew what that meant.

Supposedly, the sun didn't shine on this land, as it was forever twilight. They were lured to this world by the ringing of church bells at St. Edmund's.

Hauntings

Many of the ruined castles of England boast a ghost or two. Some of the more well-known castles, with their hauntings, are:

- Ordsall Hall, Salford (small children and John Radcliffe)
- The Tower of London (Walter Raleigh, Anne Boleyn, or The White Lady)
- Borley Rectory, Essex
- Pluckley Village, Kent (a screaming man and a highwayman pinned to a tree)
- Raynham Hall, Norfolk (the Brown Lady)
- Ancient Ram Inn, Wotton-under-Edge, Gloucestershire (built on a pagan burial ground)
- The Jamaica Inn, Cornwall (an old coaching inn, inspiration for a novel by Daphne du Maurier)
- Pendle Hill, Lancashire (the Pendle witch trials of 1612)
- Hampton Court Palace, London (two of Henry VIII's wives, Catherine Howard and Jane Seymour)
- Highgate Cemetery, London (a tall man in a hat, a shrouded figure, and other apparitions)
- Berry Pomeroy Castle, Devon (The White Lady and The Blue Lady)
- 50 Berkeley Square, London (the most haunted house in London, by a young woman who committed suicide there)
- Chillingham Castle, Northumberland (The Blue Boy and Lady Mary)
- Samlesbury Hall, Lancashire (Lady Dorothy Southworth and a group of white-clad ladies)
- Woodchester Mansion, Gloucestershire (floating coffins and a headless horseman)
- Athelhampton House, Dorset (a pair of dueling specters)
- Charleville Castle, Tullamore (a little girl)
- Arundel Castle, West Sussex (a Blue Man)

- Cannock Chase, Staffordshire (a black-eyed child)
- Dudley Castle, West Midlands (The Grey Lady, thought to be Dorothy Beaumont)
- Hellfire Caves, West Wycombe (Paul Whitehead)
- SS Great Britain, Bristol (Captain John Gray)
- The Golden Fleece Pub, York (the most haunted pub in York)

GODS AND SAINTS

People of any age hold many things sacred. They might revere holy wells, stone circles, mountain tops, ruined churches, the remains of a good person, or even just a random piece of paper.

Nowadays, folks might treasure family, money, and status. But it's a bit of a head-scratcher to figure out what exactly the ancient Britons considered sacred and why.

To make matters more complicated, traditions spread like wildfire among the neighboring populations in what is now Wales, Ireland, and Scotland. So, the lines between Celtic, Roman, Welsh, and other influences all get a bit fuzzy, and deities were being adopted and tweaked left and right across different cultures and time periods.

Oral tales were handed down from generation to generation, grandmother to grandchild. They were cherished as both history and valuable life lessons.

Kings had their own crew of bards and historians who kept this sacred knowledge alive. Those bards could pull a personal lineage or an ancient tale out of thin air with their mad memory skills.

Most of the tales, legends, beliefs, and histories we have discovered were transcribed by Christian priests, often well after the actual events. They sprinkled their Christian perspective into the mix.

Modern scholars have to use their deduction skills, outside accounts, archaeology, forensic science, and the teeny-tiny bits that survived the test of time, just to figure out what the Britons held sacred.

For instance, the Mabinogion collected loads of Welsh legends, including early versions of the classic characters Gwydion, Rhiannon, and Pwyll. But these deities are often melded into the greater Celtic pantheon along with Lugh, Brigit, and that crowd, as well as continental Gaulish entities like Epona or Cernunnos. Separating them out by present-day arbitrary borders is, if you'll excuse the reference, a Herculean task.

Be that as it may, I've tried to extract gods and goddesses that are unique to the beliefs of people who lived in what is now England. Not perfect, not comprehensive, but my best attempt.

The Britons were all about local flavor. Many of their deities were specific to a spring, river, or hill, and not widely worshipped across the land.

Regardless, the Britons held onto their beliefs with fierce determination. Here is a peek at some of those powers explained or, at least, described.

Gods and Goddesses

Because of the many layers of other cultures overlaid on the Britons, we sometimes just have names, but no legends, no attributes. We no longer have any details to flesh out the ideals that the name was attached to. While there were plenty of fairies and spirits, deities were rather thin on the rocky ground, so to speak.

Some entities who may have been revered as gods are now but names of kings in Geoffrey of Monmouth's histories, demoted from divinity by the passage of centuries.

Bran

Known in Welsh as Bendigeidfran or Bran Fendigaidd, he's a giant and a king whose lore is steeped in magic and ancient heroism. Stories tell of his epic size that allowed him to wade through seas and his magical cauldron that could resurrect the dead.

When his sister Branwen is mistreated by her Irish husband, Bran doesn't hesitate to cross the Irish Sea to rescue her, even if it leads to his own demise.

After his death, Bran's head is said to have been buried in London, facing France as a protective charm against invasion.

Brigantia

Initially revered by the Brigantes tribe in Northern England, her name suggests high status or nobility. Often associated with victory, sovereignty, and protection, Brigantia was later syncretized with the Roman goddess Minerva and North African goddess Caelestis during the Roman occupation.

Coventina

Her worship was primarily focused on water, revered as the guardian of rivers and wells near Carrawburgh on Hadrian's Wall. Offerings and dedicatory inscriptions were discovered at a well shrine.

Known for her healing and purifying powers, Coventina represents the life-giving and sustaining properties of water, a vital resource in ancient societies.

Belatucadros

This deity was predominantly worshipped in the northwestern regions of Roman Britain. Often associated with war and destruction,

Belatucadros was revered by Roman soldiers stationed along Hadrian's Wall, indicating a likely syncretism with the Roman god Mars.

Despite his martial attributes, he was also connected to the natural world, with the name Belatucadros possibly meaning "fair shining one" or "fair slayer."

Elen of the Ways

Often depicted as a guardian of pathways and, symbolically, as a guide through life's journey, Elen of the Ways is sometimes portrayed as an antlered figure. She's intimately connected with the natural world, embodying elements of wilderness.

She also has some connection with dreams and shamanic journeys. Elen's pathways are believed to represent the migratory trails of reindeer, linking her with movement, transition, and transformation.

Nantosuelta

Symbolizing abundance, domesticity, and possibly the afterlife, Nantosuelta is often depicted holding a house-shaped model, a symbol of domestic prosperity. She's linked with homesteads, fertility, and plenty.

Occasionally, Nantosuelta is shown with a raven, a creature associated with the Otherworld, suggesting a possible role as a psychopomp or guide of souls.

Sirona

In British and Gaulish mythology, Sirona is often depicted with serpents, eggs, or dogs, symbols of healing and life force. She was particularly venerated at thermal and mineral springs.

Interestingly, Sirona was syncretized with the Greek and Roman goddess of wisdom, Athena/Minerva, during the Roman occupation, linking her to wisdom and strategic warfare.

Alaunus

A god from ancient British and Gaulish mythology, Alaunus is often linked with healing, prophecy, and the sun. He's occasionally identified with the Roman god of medicine and healing, Apollo, due to their shared associations, indicating a likely syncretism during the Roman occupation of Britain.

Although specific details about Alaunus are scarce due to limited historical records, inscriptions invoking his name have been found around healing springs and sanctuaries.

Nodens

This god is primarily associated with healing, the sea, hunting, and dogs. His worship was particularly prominent at the temple complex at Lydney Park in Gloucestershire, where numerous artifacts and inscriptions related to him have been discovered.

Some interpret the name Nodens to imply catching, trapping, or snaring, linking him to hunting. It's also speculated that Nodens has connections to sleep and dreams, enhancing his healing associations.

Herne the Hunter

This entity takes many forms, from a Windsor Forest ghost, to Cernunnos, an ancient god of the Wild Hunt. He wears antlers, rides a horse, harasses herds of cattle, and rides through the darkest forest during the night.

He could have been related to the Norse god Odin, or European legends of the Wild Hunstmen. Shakespeare wrote about him in The Merry Wives of Windsor. He showed up more recently in the BBC production of Robin of Sherwood in the 1980s.

Sulis

This deity is celebrated as a goddess of healing and sacred waters. Her primary center of worship was the thermal springs at Bath, known as Aquae Sulis in Roman times, where she was revered for her healing powers.

Sulis was syncretized with the Roman goddess Minerva during the Roman occupation, linking her to wisdom and strategic warfare. Despite this fusion of identities, Sulis maintained her unique connection to water, reflecting the importance of this life-sustaining element in ancient Briton society.

Taranis

This god is associated with thunder and the forces of nature. His name, derived from the Celtic word for thunder, and his common depictions with a wheel and a thunderbolt, underscore his command over storms. During the Roman occupation, Taranis was likened to Jupiter, the Roman king of the gods and the sky, due to their shared control over weather, but he wasn't considered a leader of his pantheon.

Epona

Originating in continental Gaul, Epona is primarily associated with horses, fertility, and sovereignty. As the sole Celtic deity adopted by the Romans, Epona had an extensive following.

She is usually depicted riding or tending to horses, highlighting her role as a protector of equines. Her name, derived from the Gaulish word for horse, and her symbolic associations with fertility and power reflect the vital role horses played in ancient societies, both in practical terms and as symbols of status and wealth.

Other Gods

Obviously, listing every god or goddess that was worshipped within the land that is now England is way beyond the scope of this

book. I've tried to highlight the more popular ones, but there are hundreds, if not thousands, associated with places within the land.

Saints

Saint George

Where else can we start, but the patron saint of England? Saint George is best known for the famous legend of Saint George and the Dragon. Born to Christian parents in the late third century, George followed his father's path and became a soldier in the Roman army.

His faith led to his martyrdom under the reign of Emperor Diocletian, who enacted a series of severe persecutions against Christians. Saint George's defiance and subsequent death for his faith established his reputation as a defender of Christianity, and he was subsequently venerated as a saint.

The legend of Saint George slaying a dragon emerged much later, in the 11th century, and bears the influence of earlier pagan myths. In the most well-known version of this tale, a dragon plagues a town, and the local people, to placate the creature, offer it sheep and even their children, chosen by lottery.

When the king's daughter is selected, Saint George arrives, slays the dragon, and rescues the princess. The townsfolk abandon their paganism and embrace Christianity.

This legend symbolizes the triumph of good over evil, with Saint George's bravery and righteousness epitomizing the virtues that would come to be associated with knighthood during the Middle Ages.

Saint Augustine of Canterbury

Saint Augustine of Canterbury played a pivotal role in bringing Christianity to the Anglo-Saxons in the 6th century. Pope Gregory the Great sent the Benedictine monk to convert the pagan King Æthelberht of Kent.

Augustine's mission was successful; he baptized the king, established the bishopric of Canterbury, and became its first archbishop. His efforts laid the foundation for the Christian Church in England.

Saint Cuthbert

This saint served as a monk, bishop, and hermit, associated with the monasteries of Melrose and Lindisfarne in the 7th century. Renowned for his piety, diligence, and kindness, Cuthbert played a vital role in spiritual outreach, often journeying to remote villages to preach.

His life of asceticism and deep connection with nature, particularly birds, remain symbolic of his saintly character.

Saint Bede

Also known as the Venerable Bede, this monk was born in Northumbria in the 7th century. He is best known for his scholarly work, "Historia Ecclesiastica Gentis Anglorum" or "The Ecclesiastical History of the English People," which offers a comprehensive account of the conversion of the English people to Christianity.

Considered the father of English history, Bede's writings significantly influenced the understanding of England's religious and social development during the early Middle Ages. He was declared a Doctor of the Church by Pope Leo XIII in 1899.

Saint Thomas Becket

This saint served as the Archbishop of Canterbury from 1162 until his murder in 1170. A close friend of King Henry II, Becket's appointment was expected to consolidate the king's control over the church.

However, Becket proved to be a fervent defender of ecclesiastical rights against the king's attempts at infringement. This led to a severe conflict between the two, culminating in Becket's murder by four knights believed to be acting on the king's wishes.

Becket's violent death in his cathedral shocked Christendom, and he was quickly canonized as a martyr for the Church, becoming a symbol of resistance against unjust secular authority.

Saint Edward the Confessor

One of the last Anglo-Saxon kings of England, he reigned from 1042 to 1066 and was known for his deep religious devotion and piety.

He is perhaps best known for commissioning the construction of Westminster Abbey, which was consecrated shortly before his death and remains one of England's most iconic religious sites.

Edward is considered the patron saint of kings, difficult marriages, and separated spouses.

Saint Æthelwold of Winchester

Saint Æthelwold was a significant figure in the 10th-century monastic reform movement. He devoted himself to the reformation and standardization of monastic life based on the Rule of Saint Benedict.

He rebuilt monasteries, promoted learning, and played a vital role in the revival of monasticism in England. His "Regularis Concordia," an adaptation of the monastic rule for English monasteries, was instrumental in shaping monastic culture.

Saint Hilda of Whitby

As the founding abbess of the monastery at Whitby, she was known for her wisdom and was often consulted by kings and bishops. She played a crucial role in the Synod of Whitby in 664, which was held at her monastery and decided the calculation of Easter and other contentious issues between the Roman and Celtic branches of the church in England.

Saint Edmund the Martyr

The King of East Anglia was venerated as one of England's earliest patron saints. Known for his piety and just rule, Edmund's reign was abruptly ended in 869 or 870 when the Danes invaded England.

According to legend, when captured, Edmund refused to renounce his Christian faith or serve as a vassal to the pagan invaders, leading to his execution. The Danes reportedly tied him to a tree, shot him full of arrows, and then beheaded him.

Saint Alban

Saint Alban is celebrated as the first-recorded British Christian martyr and the patron saint of converts and refugees. Tradition holds that he was a citizen of the Roman city of Verulamium (modern-day St Albans) in the 3rd century, during a time of widespread Christian persecution.

Upon providing shelter to a Christian priest and impressed by the priest's faith, Alban converted to Christianity. When soldiers came to arrest the sheltered priest, Alban dressed in the priest's cloak and was taken in his place, subsequently suffering execution.

Summary

Without a crystal ball, we cannot know everything the ancient Britons held sacred. We can infer, we can guess, we can believe, but we cannot know. They seem to have revered powers that are attached to the land, the weather, the rivers, and the sea, forces that, to them, would have ruled their daily lives.

A poor crop, a fierce storm, a bleak winter, any of these could spell out disaster and starvation for a poor crofter, living on the edge of a rocky island. Attempting to control this fate by appealing to a higher power would have been the only option given to them.

With the advent of Christianity, this power was consolidated into the Father God, but he had many saints, or appointees, to help those "on the ground."

Many Christian priests appealed to the pagans by comparing their One True God with the pagan gods. One reason for December 25th being chosen as Christmas was to coincide with pagan rituals at Saturnalia and Winter Solstice.

Greenwich

BALLADS, SHANTIES, AND BRITCOMS

When you think of England and traditional music, some folks might think of sea shanties, or Christmas carols, or folk ballads. However, while these are an integral part of English music and national identity, there is so much more to the rich tapestry of English music and dance.

And the modern age has a wealth of English artists and talent for anyone's taste.

Types of music

Classical

Classical music is not solely the purview of continental Europe. Composers such as Henry Purcell, Edward Elgar, Ralph Vaughan Williams, Benjamin Britten, Judith Weir, and Thomas Adès all hail from England.

Folk Music

English folk music, an important part of the country's musical heritage, dates back centuries and is a reflection of the culture, history, and spirit of the people. Characterized by its distinct regional variations, the genre includes diverse forms such as dance music, ballads, lullabies, love songs, as well as moral and philosophical songs.

Traditional English folk music is often defined by its simple melodies and narratives, sometimes inspired by historical events, rural life, or love stories, with many songs passed down orally from generation to generation.

The genre saw significant revivals in the 20th century, most notably in the mid-1900s, which rejuvenated interest and introduced it to new audiences.

It also led to the creation of new subgenres such as folk rock, with bands like Fairport Convention and Steeleye Span combining elements of rock music with traditional folk. Notable artists include Bert Jansch, Nick Drake, Billy Bragg, Kate Rusby, Cat Stevens, John Martyn, Mediæval Bæbes, The Imagined Village, and Ed Sheeran.

Scrumpy and Western

Scrumpy and Western music is a unique subgenre of music that originated in the West Country of England. The term "Scrumpy" refers to a type of cloudy cider traditionally made in the region.

Scrumpy and Western music blends elements of English folk music with humorous lyrics often themed around rural life, local dialects, and the consumption of cider.

Notable bands in this genre include The Wurzels, who achieved national fame in the UK with their hit "Combine Harvester" in 1976. Despite being relatively niche, Scrumpy and Western music has a dedicated following and is a distinctive part of the West Country's cultural identity.

Rock

While America is the source of rock-n-roll, the British ran with the concept, and in the mid-1960s, there was a "British Invasion" of rock music. Early stars included Cliff Richard and, of course, The Beatles. Other notable bands include The Moody Blues, The Animals, the Rolling Stones, The Kinks, and Herman's Hermits.

As the genre grew and matured, bands such as Led Zeppelin, Cream, and Fleetwood Mac added their bluesy, psychedelic, and experimental sounds.

In the 1970s, England provided talents such as Elton John, David Bowie, The Who, and Queen. Other subgenres formed, such as Glam Rock, Progressive Rock, Heavy Metal, Punk Rock, and New

Wave. Those gave way to Gothic Rock, Dream Pop, Britpop, and New Rave.

Punk

Emerging in the mid-1970s, Punk Rock had short, fast-paced songs with hard-edged melodies and raw instrumentation. A lot of themes were rebellious against the establishment, and many were independently produced. Punk rock, though it began in the United States, created a movement that spread worldwide.

Notable artists include The Clash, Sex Pistols, Ramones, and Buzzcocks.

Electronic/Dance

Gaining ground in the 1990s, electronic music encompasses subgenres such as synthpop, techno, trance, trip hop, dubstep, and industrial. Some artists include Pet Shop Boys, Massive Attack, The Chemical Brothers, Eurythmics, Underworld, and The Prodigy.

Pop

Pop is a broad term, simply meaning "popular," but the generally has catchy lyrics and melody, and typically young, attractive singers. Bands such as Oasis, The Spice Girls, Dua Lipa, Harry Styles, Adele, and Amy Winehouse are some examples of this style, though there are so many more, too many to list here.

The Dancing

English dancing is steeped in a rich tradition that spans centuries, reflecting the evolution of the country's social and cultural landscape. From the elegant steps of courtly dances to the hearty energy of folk dances, English dance is a vibrant form of expression that continues to engage audiences.

Traditional English dance forms include country dances, Morris dancing, and maypole dancing. The country dances were extremely popular in the 17th and 18th centuries and often involved groups of couples forming geometric patterns and dancing in sequences, similar to square dancing in the United States.

Morris dance, a ritual folk dance typically performed on ceremonial occasions, is distinctive for its use of props like sticks, swords, and handkerchiefs, and is often seen at festivals.

South Downs

English dancing has taken on new dimensions with the influence of various international styles, ballet, and modern dance forms. English social dances, or "barn dances," remain popular for their inclusive, community-building spirit and often feature elements of various folk traditions.

Today's dance performances in England also encompass a wide array of genres, including hip hop, contemporary, jazz, and many more.

Ballet has a significant place in English dance culture as well, with world-renowned institutions like the Royal Ballet shaping the nation's classical dance heritage.

The diversity and adaptability of English dancing speak to the country's openness to cross-cultural influences and ongoing creative evolution.

Finding the Music

Pubs are the community living room in England. It's a place where people gather to relax, socialize, and talk about their day. Perhaps they complain about the weather, share some funny stories, toast a pint, and listen to some music.

You can find them in every size and description across the country. Do keep in mind that not all have music, not all serve food (often this stops around 8 p.m. or 9 p.m.), and none allow smoking inside (since 2006). Sometimes there is an outdoor "beer garden" to accommodate those who must light up.

Children can be welcome in the early evenings, and sometimes well-behaved dogs. While you must be eighteen to purchase alcohol, children as young as fourteen are welcome if the pub has a children's license, as long as they don't drink alcohol.

Any children must be accompanied by an adult, and may be restricted to certain areas, such as the restaurant area of the pub. Once the food is no longer served, however, the children are usually no longer allowed.

Pubs, especially in the less populated areas, might not be open during mid- afternoon hours, say between 2 p.m. and 5 p.m. Some may close for the winter season.

There are several website resources I've listed in the Appendix that might help you find the perfect pub for some lovely traditional music.

A session could mean a solo performer, a group of twenty taking turns or playing together, or anything in between. These are not usually professional performers, but locals who just love playing, and often tourists joining in. Their performances are not polished, but they are genuine in a way that set shows are not.

If you bring your own instrument and/or your voice, you will be welcome to join. Music likely won't start until around 9 or 10 p.m. each night, but do get there earlier, as space is at a premium. We prefer to find B&Bs that are within staggering distance of a pub with music, so there are no worries about drinking and driving.

Most advertised "traditional music nights" in the bigger hotels are staged performances, with dancers and singers with honed skills. They may be slick professional performers, but they're still fun.

Some of the places in Edinburgh known for good traditional music include Sandy Bell's, Royal Oak Bar and the Wee Folk Club.

Literature, Shows and Movies

Many books, television shows, and movies have made their home in England. Not only those based on the rich history of the land, but those with some fantasy or literary license. I've listed a few of them below, with a list of places where you can visit scenes from the work. While the scope of this book is not large enough to make an exhaustive list, I've listed some of my favorites.

Movies
- **Harry Potter:** The magical stories of Hogwarts was brought to life in films. The majority of the films were shot in England, England, and some in Ireland. Some English locations were Alnwick Castle, Gloucester Cathedral, Christ Church College, Leadenhall Market, and King's Cross Station.
- **Sherlock Holmes:** Most treatments of these iconic stories by Sir Arthur Conan Doyle have been filmed in England, primarily in London. The recent Guy Ritchie interpretations also include Bath and Bristol.
- **The King's Speech:** Most of this movie about King George VI was filmed in London, though parts were at Halton House, Ely Cathedral, and the Old Royal Naval College in Greenwich.
- **Pride & Prejudice:** This Jane Austen classic is another story that has been filmed multiple times, but usually in England. Anywhere in the countryside has been fair game. Chatsworth

House, Stourhead Garden, and Basildon Park have played host to recent filming.

- **Notting Hill:** As the title implies, most of this romantic comedy with Hugh Grant and Julia Roberts was filmed in the Notting Hill district of west London.
- **James Bond:** There are lots of English locations for these films, but here are a few of them.
    - **No Time to Die:** Whitehall, London.
    - **Goldeneye/The World is Not Enough/Die Another Day/ Skyfall/Spectre:** Vauxhall Cross SIS Building, London.
    - **Die Another Day:** Eden Project, Cornwall and Bourton-on-the-Water, Cotswolds.
    - **Goldfinger/Tomorrow Never Dies:** Stoke Park, Buckinghamshire.
- **Love Actually:** This iconic romantic comedy was mostly in London, including Somerset House, Downing Street, Heathrow Airport, Oxford Street, and Gabriel's Wharf. Oh, and Notting Hill.
- **Hot Fuzz:** This action-comedy is set in a fictional quaint English village, but was filmed in Somerset (The Crown Pub, Wells, Bishop's Palace), the Barn Theatre (Hertfordshire), and Hendon.
- **The Theory of Everything:** This biopic followed the life of Stephen Hawking. It was set and filmed in Cambridgeshire, London, Middlesex, and a few others. The beach scenes were at Camber Sands and the Bluebell Railway in Sussex.
- **Billy Elliot:** This powerful story about a boy who dreams of being a ballet dancer was set in Northeast England. The school scenes in this film were shot in Langley Park Primary School. Other filming locations include the Green Drive Railway Viaduct in Seaham, Tees Transporter Bridge, New Wardour Castle, and Theatre Royal in Haymarket.
- **The Full Monty:** Since this comedy-drama was set in the industrial city of Sheffield, it makes sense that the majority of filming was there. A few exterior shots were in Chesterfield, Derbyshire at the Millthorpe Working Men's Club.

Television Series

- **Downton Abbey:** A drama set in a historical English estate (Highclere Castle), exploring the lives of both the aristocratic Crawley family and their servants.
- **The Crown:** This Netflix original series dramatizes the reign of Queen Elizabeth II, filmed in various locations around the UK.
- **Doctor Who:** A long-running science fiction series, filmed in various locations but often featuring London landmarks.
- **Peaky Blinders:** A crime drama set in post-World War I Birmingham.
- **Black Mirror:** A dystopian anthology series that often features English settings and actors.
- **Broadchurch:** A crime drama set in a fictional small town in Dorset.
- **Luthor:** A psychological crime drama set in London, featuring Idris Elba.
- **Top Gear:** A highly popular car-focused series filmed around the UK and internationally.
- **Just about any Britcom ever:** There are just too many to mention, but some of my favorites are Vicar of Dibley (Turville), Fawlty Towers (Torquay), and Waiting for God (Farmoor).

Authors (Classic)

- **William Shakespeare:** A prolific author who wrote many plays and poems. He's widely regarded as the greatest writer in the English language.
- **Jane Austen**: A novelist primarily known for books such as Pride and Prejudice, Emma, and Sense and Sensibility, mostly dealing with social standings and the plight of women in a world run by the patriarchy.
- **Charles Dickens**: Some of our most beloved tales today were written by Dickens, such as Oliver Twist and A Christmas Carol. Known for portraying gritty life in Victorian London and memorable characters, he tackled many issues such as poor social or working conditions.
- **George Orwell**: Orwell's real name was Eric Arthur Blair, and wrote several dystopian novels in criticism of societal failings, such as Animal Farm and 1984.
- **Virginia Woolf:** She pioneered the use of stream of consciousness as a narrative device, and wrote books such as Orlando, A Room of one's Own, and Dalloway.
- **J. R. R. Tolkien:** A professor at Oxford, Tolkien was a linguist and philologist. His high fantasy works The Hobbit and Lord of the Rings defined the entire genre.
- **Agatha Christie:** Still the best-selling author other than the Bible and Shakespeare, Christie defined the mystery genre. Movies and shows are still made from her books.
- **Emily Bronte:** Her novel, Wuthering Heights, is an enduring classic and portrayed mental and physical abuse in a new light for her time. She published poetry with her sisters Charlotte and Anne, well known in their own right.
- **C. S. Lewis:** A close friend of J.R.R. Tolkien's, Lewis wrote The Chronicles of Narnia, an eternal classic for young adults. He also wrote many books with a spiritual bent, such as Mere Christianity and Miracles.

Authors (Modern)

- **J. K. Rowling:** Known for writing the "Harry Potter" series, which has become the best-selling book series in history.
- **Ian McEwan:** A highly regarded contemporary novelist, his works include "Atonement," "Amsterdam," and "Enduring Love."
- **Neil Gaiman:** A prolific author known for his work in various genres, including fantasy, horror, and children's literature. His notable works include "American Gods," "Coraline," and "The Sandman" graphic novels.
- **Zadie Smith:** Gained fame with her debut novel "White Teeth." She is also known for "On Beauty" and "Swing Time."
- **Hilary Mantel:** She is the first woman to win the Man Booker Prize twice, for her novels "Wolf Hall" and "Bring Up the Bodies," part of a trilogy about Thomas Cromwell.
- **Kazuo Ishiguro:** Born in Japan, but moved to England at a young age, he has written several acclaimed novels, including "The Remains of the Day" and "Never Let Me Go." He won the Nobel Prize in Literature in 2017.
- **Philip Pullman:** He is best known for his "His Dark Materials" trilogy, which includes "The Golden Compass," "The Subtle Knife," and "The Amber Spyglass."
- **Jeanette Winterson:** Her first book, "Oranges Are Not the Only Fruit," won her the Whitbread Prize for First Novel. Her other works include "Sexing the Cherry" and "Written on the Body."
- **Sarah Waters:** Known for her novels set in Victorian society and featuring lesbian protagonists, such as "Tipping the Velvet" and "Fingersmith."
- **Kate Atkinson:** She has gained fame with both her standalone novels and her series featuring detective Jackson Brodie. Her books include "Life After Life," "A God in Ruins," and "Case Histories."

Exeter

STUNNING SHOTS

How better to capture the moment, the memory, the mood, than to take a photograph of the stunning vista laid out before your eyes in England?

One of the eternal draws of this island to millions of tourists is the beautiful sights which are everywhere, and it takes very little time (if any) to travel from one stunning landscape to the next. It's all contained in a compact, charming package, ready to share with your envious loved ones.

Photographs provide a great service to both the photographer, and his friends and family. They record the memory to share and to relive later. There are many times I've looked back on my photos and remembered a scene I had forgotten, relived a memory I had lost.

This is also a reason I write my trip reports in such detail, I know my own memory is rather faulty, so I jot down notes every time I sit down to eat during the trip. This helps me write down the narrative later and keeps my memory strong years afterwards. It also helps me realize where I took some of the photographs.

The Preparation
While there may be a few out there still using film, most people take digital photographs now, and most of those use their phone rather than a camera. If you are still on film, then some of this advice must be adjusted for this fact, so keep this in mind.

However, one of the biggest advantages of digital photography is the ability to take as many photographs as you have memory space for, and sort later the ones you wish to spend money on printing.

Most folks use their phones to take photos now. And to be fair, phone cameras have improved in leaps and bounds, and are often better than a regular digital camera. However, keep in mind that memory capacity might be an issue.

Some folks, like me, still prefer to carry a regular camera. I sell large-format prints, so I still like to use my 83X optical zoom.

I'm not much of a movie-taker, but some people prefer video to photographs. If so, much of this will also apply to the video recorder shopping. Again, if you use your phone, that doesn't apply.

The Equipment

Not everyone needs or wants a professional grade camera. These can cost over $5,000, and most people don't have this in the budget. Even high-grade amateur cameras, which usually run between $400 and $1,000, are outside most people's budget and desire.

However, a decent amateur camera can be gotten for about $150-$200, and, in my opinion, are well worth the investment. You should, however, do your research, and decide which camera is right for you. If you are not planning on printing your photographs in huge sizes for hanging on the wall, your smartphone camera should be sufficient.

There is an excellent site at Digital Photograph Review which allows you to choose cameras by feature and compare them side by side. I have used it many times to choose my next piece of equipment. You will need to decide which features are important to you.

Since I take a lot of landscape shots, and often from the window of a moving car, long optical zoom and fast shutter speed are very important to me. The ability to shoot in RAW format (which doesn't let the camera do any editing of the image) is also important to me, as I do a lot of post-production manipulation in Photoshop.

Is low light photography important to you, for night shots or party shots? How about close-ups for flowers and other macro photography? Once you know what is important, you are ready to choose a decent camera.

By the way, some of the best shots I've taken have been from a point-and-shoot $80 camera. Good equipment is helpful but is NOT essential. The art is truly in the eye of the artist, not the equipment they use.

The Accessories

Many cameras come with interchangeable lenses, one for macro, one for zoom, etc. The higher-end professional cameras have this as a matter of course. The point-and-shoots do not, for the most part. The rest of us are in the middle. My camera of choice right now is the Nikon CoolPix P900, which does NOT have a removable lens. The installed lens can zoom 83X, which means it can get decent moon shots and decent macro shots. I'm happy with this range and would rather not mess with multiple lenses.

This is my personal choice, and it may not be yours, so experiment with a few. Go to the store, pick up the camera with all its accessories. Do you want to be hiking up a mountain and through an airport, carrying all this? Or is it worth it to you?

Memory, memory, memory, without it, you are done with your digital diary. Uploading to the cloud might not always be practical. There are several options to make sure you have enough on your trip.

Memory sticks of any type are pretty cheap. My option this last trip was simply to take enough sticks to make sure I never ran out of room. I never came close, even after 9,900 photos.

I always, always, however, take at least one more than I think I will need, in case one gets corrupted or lost. Another option I've done in the past is take a laptop and download the card each night. This is fine if you are already planning on taking a laptop, not so much if you'd rather not carry the extra weight.

If you are staying at a place with good Wi-Fi, you might upload to the cloud each night, but some sites have memory caps and uploading hundreds of photos and videos does take time and bandwidth.

It's worth a note to say if you do, for some reason, accidentally erase the photos from your card, don't despair. Also, don't touch it. Don't try to take more pictures with it, save it until you can get in touch with an expert; he/she should be able to get most of the data from it.

My friend Carla did this on our trip to Scotland, 1,200 photos erased in the blink of an eye. She held on to it, and when she returned, she was able to get back about 90% of those precious memories she captured with the help of a data recovery specialist.

The Method

England is truly a land of wonders. It is not a large place, but it is packed with stunning seascapes, rolling hills, charming manor houses, romantic ruins, and bucolic pastures.

The last time I went to England, over the course of two weeks, I'd racked up over 7,000 photos. I believe in the theory you take as many photos as you possibly can on-site, as you can always sift through them later. Different perspectives, different lighting, and different levels, a couple will turn out well.

You can't as easily go back and revisit the site. Even the few times I have revisited a place and took a photograph, I've discovered the landscape has changed. Traveling to Whitby in 2000, and then again in 2008, parts of it looked completely different due to construction, time, and weather.

In England, you are tempted to stop every five minutes on your journey to take a photo of the lamb nursing by the side of the road, the ruins on the hill, or the charming, thatched cottage on the road. Go ahead and do it.

Do it safely, mind you. There are usually small lay-bys (pullouts) which you can turn into for a very short period (don't park there, they are for passing, not parking), or driveways you can turn into. This is a country made for photo opportunities, after all. After you've seen your hundredth sheep or so, you may be less tempted to stop at the sight of each one.

You should keep in mind some basic photography truths, but also keep in mind these are rules, and rules are sometimes meant to be broken.

- The rule of thirds: composition is more interesting when objects and horizon lines are on the top or bottom third of the picture, or the left/right third.
- Lines: Roads, fences, and other lines lead the eye into a particular spot, make sure the spot has something interesting.
- Scale: The mountain photo is great, but how big is it? Take a shot with a flower, tree, or cottage in the foreground to lend a perspective of scale.
- Weather: The weather in England is part of the landscape. Use it to your advantage. There's a storm coming in, wouldn't a dark cloud look dramatic over the castle? Move your body until you can get the shot lined up right. And then run for the car before the deluge hits.
- Perspective: More interesting points of view can change the feel of a photo. Shooting straight up on a castle wall or a tree, or down on a flower can work wonders.
- Action: A standing sheep is lovely, but getting a lamb while it nurses, or a pony while running makes the photo much more interesting.
- Lighting: Sunrise and sunset, storms and clouds, and the ever-present mists of England can make some amazing atmospheric shots. One reason I like staying in one place for several days is to

have several opportunities to take photos at different times of the day and night.

The Locations

While all of England is picturesque and charming, and different people like different things, there are certain places, subjects and areas which stand out as being incredibly photogenic.

- **Cliffs:** England is rugged and rough in its landscape and has a long and varied coastline. My favorite place in the world is to be on a sea cliff, looking down at the ocean crashing upon the rocks far below me. I love the mix of sea, wind, and earth, and I feel like I'm standing on the edge of the earth. As a result, I take many of my photographs in such spots. Whether it is the White Cliffs of Dover or Glebe Cliffs at Tintagel, I love the places where the water meets the land.

- **Water:** Lakes and rivers have coastlines as well, and England certainly has its share of picturesque places along its waterways. Many large lakes, such as Windermere, Ullswater, or Bassenthwaite, have stunning scenery to capture.

- **Castles:** England has hundreds of castles, ranging from grand palaces which will rent you a room for the night, to crumbling ruins which barely hold a full wall against the tide of time. Each castle is unique and has photographic charm of its own. Some areas are more castle-rich than others, such as Sussex, but there are random ruins wherever you go. Some seemingly don't even have a name, it being lost in time. Today, they are just a nuisance to the local farmer who cannot farm this part of the land.

- **Critters:** Sheep, cows, goats, donkeys, chickens, and horses. There are others, but these are what I see most of in England. Sheep, and some more sheep. And look, there are some sheep. And a horse. And more sheep. If you visit in April or May, you will see adorable lambs running after their mothers, looking for lunch.

- **Cities:** London is a jewel in the crown of the world, with beautiful architecture, but don't discount York, Oxford, or Bath. York has a rich heritage and a plethora of historic buildings, as well as the fabulous York Minster. Oxford is known as the "City of Dreaming Spires" and houses one of the most famous universities in the world. And Bath is filled with Georgian architecture and Roman sites.

- **Flowers:** England has many incredible gardens, ranging from the Royal Botanic Gardens, Kew in London to the gardens at Sissinghurst Castle in Kent or Stourhead in Wiltshire. Most cottages and houses have small, well-tended flower gardens in their homes, and the English take great pride in these miniature beauties.

- **Cottages:** Nestled in the verdant quilt of the English countryside, the humble cottage stands as a symbol of rustic serenity. Its stone walls, kissed by the passage of time, echo with stories of yesteryears, whispered on the breeze that rustles through the ivy clinging tenderly to its facade.

- **People:** Ever friendly, the people of England are usually game for posing for a photograph. Often, after a few pints in a pub, they'll not say no. Do be respectful, though, these folk are trying to go about their day, and some are quite busy with their lives.

- **Stones:** Yes, stones. England is a very rocky country. And while the cliffs are made of stone, so are the Neolithic burial sites, the stone circles, and the barrows. There is great texture and pattern in stones of all types. The north, in particular, has many of these, but they dot the entire land.

- **Churches:** Lovely churches both in Anglican and Catholic flavors are everywhere. In addition, hundreds of abbeys, both ruined and restored, are open for exploration. Larger communities may have temples or churches of other faiths, such as Muslim, Jewish, Methodist, etc. All of them are an important part of the cultural and physical landscape of the land.

Whatever you do, do NOT be afraid of walking off the beaten path. Climb into the forest, up a rock, into a graveyard, around a stone wall, the possibilities are endless.

Of course, be aware of your surroundings and dress appropriately for your adventures. Bring what supplies are required, such as walking sticks, sturdy shoes, water and food, etc.

If you are truly adventurous, go on a mountain walk (please, with an experienced guide). Keep in mind some sites are only accessible if you walk THROUGH someone's yard or field. This is allowed but do be respectful with the owners' permission (as this may be a working farm or other place of business) and do no harm to the property.

The Aftermath

Inevitably, you get home and look at your photos, and you are disappointed. You remember it being much more breathtaking than the photo could capture. This is, unfortunately, due to the limitations of modern technology.

While today's cameras are incredible, they still are not the human eye, and can only capture a thin slice of the wonder we see with our own incredibly complex eye structure. Even the eye cannot truly see all our mind imagines when we look upon a fantasy landscape like England. Our imagination fills the faery hills and standing stones with mystery and wonder. Our eye only sees part of this, and the camera captures even less of it.

One of the reasons I unapologetically manipulate my photographs is I want to share what my mind saw at the location, not what my eye saw, or what the camera captured. I want to share this with those who couldn't be there to experience it with me. It's a tall order and sometimes very difficult to accomplish, but I work at it until I am mostly satisfied with my results.

I usually print my photos in small format first, to see how they come out in that format (the computer screen sometimes isn't the best portrayal of print photograph). I then order the prints larger to sell.

I use a company called White House Custom Copies. You can upload your photos to their server and receive them a couple days later. I've never had a problem with WHCC, and their customer service is top-notch. I've also printed canvas prints with Simply Canvas, and books and calendars at Lulu. There are many ways to share your memories with those you love.

PINTS AND FISH & CHIPS

England has long had a reputation for boring and tasteless food. The joke goes that they explored the world over to find all the exotic spices, only to ignore them.

However, after a while they realized that they had a wealth of natural game, produce and spices, and stopped exporting all the yummy stuff. England experienced a renaissance in cuisine and now take great pride in it.

Now, you can get a great nosh at food trucks and take-away places, but the high-end restaurants will not leave you wanting. Takeaway is a great way to experience fantastic ethnic food. Some of the best Indian food I've ever had was at English take-away joint in Chiswick, and a fantastic sit-down Turkish restaurant in Soho.

Breakfasts

If you are staying at Bed & Breakfasts (B&Bs), you will be served a fantastic breakfast by your hosts. One option is almost always the Full English Breakfast, also known as the *All-Day Breakfast*:

- This starts off with an egg (usually fried, but it can often be poached or scrambled by choice).
- Then a bit of fried or grilled bacon is added. This is not like American bacon, it's more like a slice of fatty ham, much thicker than ours, almost a fattier version of Canadian Bacon. They call our type of bacon "streaky bacon."

- Add a couple of link sausage, these are usually not very spicy or peppery.
- Black pudding, a slice of sausage made with grains, spices, and pigs' blood.
- White pudding, like black pudding, but without the blood, and made with different spices.
- Grilled half tomato.
- Grilled mushrooms.
- Baked beans.
- Fried bread (sliced white bread fried in the oil used to prepare the rest of the breakfast).

Other options may include smoked salmon with scrambled eggs, porridge (aka oatmeal), various cold cereals, fresh and stewed/canned fruit, poached eggs.

In addition, most places offer coffee, tea, milk, and often several types of juice. Sometimes there are homemade jams and jellies, scones, or pancakes as well. Occasionally, I've had muesli, or a mixed fruit/grain/cream concoction that was delicious.

Now you know why the Full English Breakfast is also called the All-Day Breakfast. You will NOT go away hungry from an English breakfast, and most likely, you won't be hungry again until 2 or 3pm, at which point, most places will no longer be serving lunch. So, eat less and have a normal lunchtime, or be prepared with snacks to keep you until dinner.

Food

Western civilization is extremely food oriented. We meet for lunch; we meet for drinks. If we have someone over as a guest, we offer them a drink, and we sit down for a dinner party. Barbecues and picnics are how families meet up. We obsess about our weight, our presentation, the taste, style, and healthiness of food, everything associated with the act of eating. So how do the English do all of this?

My restaurant of choice in England (or anywhere else in Great Britain or Ireland) is the pub. Sometimes this is because it's the only thing open at 2 or 3 p.m. serving food by the time I've worked off the huge English Breakfast. Also, the food is fairly inexpensive, and Gastropubs have raised the bar on quality food.

Traditionally, pubs have been primarily for drinking, with a packet of crisps (potato chips), pork scratching (pork rinds), or peanuts as an afterthought. Some pubs served "pies and a pint," the pies being meat and potatoes encased in pastry and baked and held in the hand to eat.

Now, traditional pub grub can include those same meat pies, plus hearty stews, fish & chips, carvery roasts, and whatever the pub's chef can conjure up on the day. A Ploughman's Lunch (bits of cheese, relish or pickle, leftover carved roast from the previous day, and some bread) is a holdover from this time.

While many pubs have their own signature meals on their menu, there are certain dishes you will usually always find at almost any pub worth its salt in England.

- **Fish & chips:** Originally brought to the British Isles by Italian immigrants, this dish has become synonymous with England, Wales, Ireland, and Scotland. Flaky white fish (usually cod or whiting) is battered and deep fried and served thick-cut chips (fries). Often served with salt and vinegar or tartar sauce.

- **Mussels:** Especially in coastal areas, mussels are a staple, most often served in a white wine and garlic sauce, and a side of traditional brown bread and butter.
- **Steak & ale pie:** A thick, dark savory type of stew loaded with chunks of beef, potato, carrot baked in a flaky pastry, I've also seen it with lamb, known as lamb and ale pie.
- **Deep fried mushrooms:** Coated in batter or crumbs, and deep fried. Often with aioli sauce/garlic mayo for dipping.
- **Goat's cheese salad:** Sometimes the cheese is coated in crumbs then fried, sometimes baked, sometimes cold. Usually served on salad greens with a sweet chutney of some sort, like berry compote.
- **Shepherd's Pie:** Savory minced/ground lamb and vegetables topped with mashed potatoes and baked until the potatoes are golden. Cottage Pie is most often offered in tourist establishments. This is the same as Shepherd's Pie but is made with beef rather than lamb.
- **Burgers:** Yes, lots of burgers. Those served in upscale eateries are made with high-quality beef and lots of topping choices. Take-aways also offer burgers on their menu, which are highly processed. Chicken sandwiches are becoming very popular.
- **Smoked salmon:** Usually served with traditional brown bread and butter, perhaps some capers or dill dressing.
- **Curry & chips:** Try it. I was skeptical at first, but curry makes an excellent sauce for your chips.
- **Prawn cocktail with Marie Rose sauce:** Unlike the tomatoey sauce in America, Marie Rose sauce is made from mayonnaise and ketchup, sometimes with a little Worcestershire Sauce. Small prawns are added to the sauce and mixed well, then served on a bed of lettuce or in a small bowl.
- **Steak and Kidney Pie:** A traditional British pie made from steak and kidney, cooked in a gravy and wrapped in a flaky pastry.
- **Mushy Peas:** This side dish is served with lots of meals, almost by default. It's similar to a very thick split pea soup, but without the chunks of ham or bacon. Occasionally, there is mint added.

- **Chicken Tikka Masala:** While its origins are disputed, this dish is incredibly popular in the UK. It consists of roasted marinated chicken chunks in a spiced curry sauce.
- **Sunday Roast:** This traditional meal typically includes roasted meat, potatoes, Yorkshire pudding, vegetables, and gravy.
- **Cornish Pasty:** A type of pie originating from Cornwall, traditionally filled with beef, potatoes, swede, and onions.
- **Bangers & Mash:** Sausage and mashed potatoes, what can be better?
- **Toad in the Hole:** A sausage baked in a Yorkshire pudding, covered in gravy.
- **Sticky toffee pudding:** A steamed sponge cake made with chopped dates, covered in a butter rum toffee sauce, usually served warm.
- **Bread and butter pudding:** Traditional bread pudding, made with chunks of stale bread in an eggy-custardy mix with cinnamon or all spice, most often with raisins, and served with a whisky sauce, and warm pouring custard on the side.
- **Spotted Dick:** A traditional British pudding made with suet and dried fruit, often served with custard.
- **Trifle:** A dessert with layers of sponge cake, jelly, fruit, custard, and whipped cream.
- **Eton Mess:** A dessert made of broken meringue, strawberries, and whipped cream, traditionally served at Eton College's annual cricket game.
- **Bannoffee Pie:** As the name implies: banana and toffee made into a creamy pie. Onto a cookie crumb base, fresh sliced bananas are layered, then the creamy banana-toffee cream is poured on and refrigerated until set. It's served with generous lashings of fresh whipped cream and drizzles of toffee sauce on top, and chocolate shavings, and sometimes chopped fresh nuts.

Some pubs have different items, of course, and the fancier they want to look, the more haute they try to make their cuisine. I've seen a couple failed efforts here and there, but for the most part, the Gastropubs (and even those regular pubs that care) do a pretty good job firing up the food.

If you would rather not eat at the pub, the "normal" restaurants are great, as well. I'm a big fan of seafood, and England has wonderful dishes made with salmon, prawns, mackerel, mussels, scallops, oysters, and anything else you can imagine. English beef is top-notch, but I usually go for the lamb, as it is more difficult to find in the US, and it is everywhere on the menu in England.

Ethnic restaurants tend to be delicious as well, some of the best Turkish, Indian, and Chinese food I've had has been in England.

Street food is also a great option, I've had pancakes (crepes), fish & chips, chips and curry, and gyros served roadside in mobile food vans. Or you can get supplies at the grocery store and snack on the road.

Bonus tip: If you are staying in a self-catering place, you will have a full kitchen to make your own creations.

Here are some other traditional treats you might find and try:

- **Scones with Clotted Cream and Jam:** Similar to American biscuits, these are usually made sweet, with bits of date, raisins (sultanas) or other fruit inside. I've occasionally seen savory scones with cheese or rosemary, as well.

- **Beef Wellington:** This dish consists of a filet steak coated with pâté and duxelles, which is then wrapped in puff pastry and baked.
- **Bubble and Squeak:** A dish made from boiled potatoes and cabbage, mixed together and then fried.
- **Lancashire Hotpot:** A slow-cooked stew from Lancashire, typically made with lamb, onions, and potatoes.
- **Gammon Steak:** Typically served with eggs or pineapple, this is a classic English dish.
- **Mince Pies:** Small pies filled with a mixture of dried fruits and spices known as "mincemeat," that are traditionally served around Christmas.
- **Victoria Sponge Cake:** Named after Queen Victoria, this cake is a sandwich of two sponge cakes, with a layer of raspberry jam and whipped double cream or vanilla cream in the middle.
- **Eccles Cake:** Small, round cakes filled with currants and made from flaky pastry with butter.
- **Jellied Eels:** A traditional English dish that originated in the 18th century, primarily in the East End of London. The dish consists of chopped eels boiled in a spiced stock, the latter of which is allowed to cool and set, forming a jelly.

Indian restaurants are very popular in England, as the British ruled over India for almost a hundred years. During that time, many Indians emigrated to the British Isles, and made lives there. They brought their spices and palates to awaken local sensibilities to the wonders of Indian food.

Here are a few of the restaurants I've enjoyed throughout England during my trips.

TAS, a Turkish restaurant in London, served us a delightful meal of TAS Iskender, which is basically a mixed grill on bread with tomato sauce and yogurt.

Although I believe it's now closed, we had several fantastic meals at the Rat & Parrot Pub in Chiswick, London. The chef at the time was Australian, and I had the most delicious Persian lamb casserole, which was spicy and sweet, tomato-based but with cinnamon and cardamon.

The White Hart Inn in East Drayton was a port in the storm for us, the only place still serving food at 9pm, when we arrived in town after a long travel day. We had delightfully savory meat pies with thick gravy. It might have been hunger, it might have been jet lag, but they tasted like ambrosia.

Since we tend to favor pubs for lunch, we enjoyed the Rose and Crown pub in Nottingham and enjoyed chicken with mushrooms and gravy.

Another London place we visited was Stephano's Grill, a Lebanese/Italian establishment with lamb shawarma, hummus, and chicken curry.

Another lovely pub was the Coach & Horses in Carlisle. We had fried mushrooms and a steak and ale pie, with gravy to dip my chips in.

When we were staying near York, we found a pub called the Fox & Grapes. I had lamb moussaka, sort of like a potato-based lasagna with eggplant and lamb.

Another nearby place was Nawab, an Indian restaurant several blocks from our B&B. We had samosas, lamb haandi, and chicken jalfrasi. It also had a dessert new to us called Fantastica, which was caramel and vanilla ice cream with toffee and chocolate on top.

When we stayed in Leeds, we found a Chinese restaurant called 56 Oriental, an upscale noodle bar. I had a dish with scallops, shrimp, chicken, duck, and veggies in an oyster sauce.

Drinks

England has a rich history of beverages, both alcoholic and non-alcoholic.

- **Tea:** Perhaps the most iconic drink of them all, the British are known for their love of tea. Whether it's black tea, Earl Grey, or English Breakfast, it's often enjoyed with a splash of milk and perhaps some sugar.
- **Pimm's:** A fruit cup, but most commonly associated with its No. 1 Cup, a gin-based beverage mixed with lemonade and various

fruits, herbs, and spices. It's particularly popular in the summer and during Wimbledon.

- **Ale/Bitter:** Traditional English ales are distinct and have been brewed for centuries. There are many regional variations, with many breweries producing their unique flavors and styles.
- **Stout (like Guinness):** While Guinness is Irish, stouts and porters have a long history in England as well.
- **Gin:** England, particularly London, has a storied history with gin. From the gin craze in the 18th century to the modern craft gin movement, it's been a favorite spirit for many.
- **Cider:** Particularly popular in the West Country (like Somerset and Herefordshire), English ciders are often less sweet than some international versions.
- **Blackcurrant Cordial (Ribena):** A sweet concentrate made from blackcurrants, it's often diluted with water to make a refreshing drink. It became popular during World War II when oranges were scarce, and vitamin C from blackcurrants was promoted instead.
- **Lemon Barley Water:** A traditional non-alcoholic drink made from barley, lemon, and sugar. Historically, it's been associated with Wimbledon, where it was a favored refreshment for players.
- **Buck's Fizz:** Similar to a mimosa, it's a cocktail made with equal parts champagne and orange juice. It's often consumed at celebrations or during brunch.
- **Shandy:** A mix of beer and lemonade (or another non-alcoholic drink). It provides a refreshing, low-alcohol option for a hot day.

Obviously, there isn't room for a list of all the drinks you might find in England, either at the pub or at afternoon tea. But this should give you a taste (if you'll pardon the pun) of what you can get.

Jervaulx Abbey, Yorkshire

PLANS AND MECHANICS

When you plan a trip somewhere, there are all sorts of facets to your planning. Each facet requires your attention, and ignoring one could be potentially upsetting, inconvenient, or worse. This section should help with the practical aspects of planning and enjoying a trip to England. Here are some of the things I shall cover:

How do I plan a trip to England? When do I go?
How much will it cost? Where will I stay?
How will I get around? What shall I visit?
What if something goes wrong?

Many folks dream about the magic of England. However, many do not grab this dream. Why not? "It's too expensive," you say. "I could never afford a trip to Europe."

Less expensive than a week at Disneyworld, I say. For six people on a three-week England vacation in June (2008), including airfare, rental car, B&B accommodation and trip insurance, we spent about $2,600 per person. Yes, that's it.

Now, this doesn't include food, petrol (gasoline) or souvenirs, of course, but it did include a wonderful vacation to a *truly* magical place.

Also, prices change all the time, especially for airfare. 2008 was many years ago, and prices are obviously higher for everything now. Any information I publish on hard airfare numbers will be obsolete by the time you read it, but I can and will give examples below.

So, how do you get such a deal? Well, it takes patience, research, and the ability to make decisions when you need to. I will take you through, step-by-step, how to get the best deal for an English vacation.

DECISIONS: Why, Who, What, Where, When, and How

Why?

You should start by thinking about WHY you want to go to England. Do you want to touch the roots of your ancestors? Or experience an ancient culture? Have you always felt an unexplainable pull? Or do you just want to get away from the screaming kids, or make your co-workers jealous? There are many reasons WHY you may want to go to England. No need to pick one. Pick several. Use these reasons to help plan your trip.

Who?

WHO's going? You? Your spouse? Your children or parents? Your best friend? A huge group of twenty friends? This decision makes a big difference in accommodation and transportation choices. I have learned, through trial and many errors, that there are certain people who travel well together, and those who don't. For instance, I will no longer travel with a mixed group of friends, spouse, and/ or family. I have determined, in order to keep my sanity, I shall only travel with one type of companion at a time. Otherwise, I become a funnel through which all complaints about others are poured. Choose wisely to avoid problems.

What?

WHAT to do? Are you interested in touring the pubs? Ruined or restored castles and abbeys? Cities or charming villages? Your trip doesn't have to have a theme, of course, but it is more fun if you do, and helps you to plan when your mind is a blank.

Perhaps you've seen a movie or read a book set in Yorkshire, and want to visit the area? Or maybe you dance and want to learn Morris Dancing, or you play an instrument and want to learn how to play the lute? There is so much to see and do in England that your imagination can take flight.

Where?

WHERE to go, of course, depends on WHAT you are doing. It also ties into WHEN you want to go. It probably needs to be considered as a package deal, so to speak.

WHERE includes the character of place: Towns and villages, or bustling city? Mountains or patchwork hills? Coastline or the Lake District? Each city has its own character, and a variety of places to stay, from historic B&Bs to luxury hotels.

English cities are compact so choose accommodation with parking, as you won't need the car, as most things are within walking distance. Villages used as a base of exploration can be wonderful, and you get more chances to meet the locals.

Urban, suburban, or rural, you will be spoiled for choice. More details on this decision are explored under "WHY?" below.

When?

WHEN is an important consideration. While the weather is, on average, nicer in the summer, and the days are longer, the trip will also be more expensive and more crowded.

Alternatively, while the winter is cheaper and you have things more to yourself, the weather is harsher. Most traditional tourist attractions will be closed or some natural sites inaccessible in poor weather. Also, the days will be much shorter with an average of seven hours of daylight. It's up to you to determine your comfort zone.

The peak season is June, July, and August. The shoulder seasons of March, April, and May, and September, October, and November may offer the best of both worlds, and is my preferred time for traveling.

Except for right around Christmas and Easter, the winter months, December through February, offer the best deals, but also the highest possibility of weather difficulties and limited open attractions.

How?

HOW are you going to get there, and HOW will you get around once you are there? Usually, the easiest answer to the former question is via airplane. Airfare will be a good chunk of your travel budget, but with some research and patience, you can find a decent fare.

Keep in mind that some websites quote the base fare with taxes, and then have additional fees, so make sure you are comparing apples to apples when doing your research. While there are now regulations set to have the total fare (including taxes) displayed, that won't include baggage fees and other optional add-ons.

There are several sites I go to in order to find comparable flights, such as the airlines themselves, but also Kayak and Googleflights. The cost is usually higher from smaller airports, and from those farther away, such as California, as compared to east coast departures.

And check the most direct flights to save on travel time and fewer connections. For example: California to London Heathrow, total flight time around ten hours direct. But if you have a layover in, say, Newark, that adds a couple hours of flight time as well as the layover, which could be three or four hours.

The latter question, of how to travel once you are on the ground, has more options. While my favorite, by far, is to rent my own car and wander around the moors and hills on my own, this is not the only option.

You can travel to some of the main destinations by train or even by ferry or go via tour bus (either an all-inclusive tour or shorter day trips). You can also hike or cycle. You can even combine methods of travel, such as drive or train to Berwick-upon-Tweed and get the ferry to Lindisfarne.

Since COVID-19, costs of many things have gone up, so everything is still in flux. Rental cars, in particular, have skyrocketed, due to companies selling off excess inventory during the pandemic. I recommend researching early, reserving early, and check often to ensure you have a good deal.

Renting A Car

The first thing to remember is that all rentals have compulsory insurances included in the rental rate. These minimum insurances include CDW (Collision Damage Waiver), VTP (Vehicle Theft Protection), LLI (Limited Liability Insurance), and location surcharges, as well as the cost of the rental itself and VAT (Value Added Tax).

Understand what each of these insurances pay and consider optional insurances on collection, which include PLI (Personal Liability Insurance), SCDW (Super CDW), TPI (Third Party Insurance), and T&WC (Tyre/Tire and Windscreen/Windshield Coverage).

CDW covers damage to the vehicle. Period. If you're in an accident, this compulsory insurance repairs or replaces the vehicle (most CDW coverage only pays up to 80-90% of damages and the renter covers the balance).

SCDW is the same as CDW but covers that percentage which is left over from traditional CDW coverage. This covers 100% of the vehicle.

If you're in an accident and there are injuries, LLI will pay medical costs for those injured if you hit another vehicle. It will not pay for those injured in your vehicle. PLI covers injured passengers in your vehicle.

CDW/SCDW and LLI/PLI are often covered as part of your travel insurance package. If they are, you do not have to buy them again as part of the vehicle rental contract. Be sure to bring a copy of your travel insurance with you for proof upon picking up your rental vehicle.

T&WC is not compulsory insurance, but one you should consider adding on. As part of the standard rental contract, if you puncture a tire or a stone cracks the windscreen, you are responsible for repair, which can be as much as £100 for a tire and £500 for the windscreen. Adding T&WC onto your contract will pay these damages so you don't have to.

Read the fine print when getting rental quotes online. Some companies do include more than the basic insurances in their quote.

Most credit cards issued in the US will cover travel insurance on vehicles rented in England. However, many of them have a value cap of $50,000 for the rented vehicle (this largely applies to luxury models).

Depending on the size of car you rent and the exchange rate that day, it may be that the car you rent is over that cap, and thus the credit card will not cover it. Also, cars might be more expensive there than the same car would be here. Do your research and be prepared.

If you do not have travel insurance coverage on your credit card, you might be able to buy it as part of your travel insurance. Check out *Insure My Trip* online to see your options.

Also, if you get coverage from someone other than the rental company, be aware they may put either a hold on your credit card for several thousand pounds, or actually charge a deposit to the card, which is refunded when you return the car in good order.

While this sounds like the same thing, it is not, as many credit cards charge a 2-3% foreign transaction fee for any transaction. This would be charged twice for a deposit and a subsequent refund, so you would be out this fee twice. Do some research ahead of time to see if this is the policy of the rental agency, their rules can change at any time.

RESEARCH:
Find out everything about everything, then throw half of it away.

The internet is many things. Addicting, yes; maddening, yes. But it is also incredibly helpful when doing research, especially about places far from your home. Airfare, accommodation, car rental, and destinations like cities, beautiful beaches (yes, they exist in England), and gloomy castles are all listed somewhere, you just have to find them. The best order of research I've found is as follows:

- Make up a crazy wish list, anything you (and your traveling companions) have any interest in seeing.
- Decide which items are your "must-sees," those places you have your heart set on.
- Plot out these "must-sees" on a map of England.
- See if you can construct a basic progressive itinerary from those spots, incorporating the "non-must-sees" when you can, trying not to double back on yourself.

- See if you can find airfare in and out of places logical for the itinerary.
- Research accommodation along the way.
- Research ground transportation.

The airfares available may define your itinerary somewhat, and the itinerary will help define other items. Just try staying flexible.

Itinerary

There is a wealth of information online about places to see: castles and manor houses, museums and historical monuments, special interest workshops, battle sites, and many other places of interest.

Most cities and towns, even villages, have their own website with tourist information. In addition, many travel agent websites have great information for the intrepid traveler.

Even more, there are websites dedicated to those interested in travel, with wonderful forums for those odd questions. Some of my favorites are listed in the Maps and Resources section at the back of this book.

Once you have done exhaustive research of the places you want to see, throw half of it out. Yes, that's right, you will likely end up with a list of seventeen things to see in each location, but you will only have time for a third of them, so pick your favorites.

I usually list about twice as many as I can possibly see and bold the ones I REALLY want to see. That way, if, for some reason, I have extra time (say, one of my must-sees was closed, or didn't take as long as I had thought it would), I can see some of my second-string choices.

Also, do yourself a favor by leaving room in your itinerary for free time, wandering around and getting lost, people-watching at a café, or just having a pint with the locals.

These are usually the most memorable parts of your trip, so leave time for them. You don't want to end up with an itinerary where you are rushing through things so fast you don't see them.

While some people prefer a fast-paced vacation, it does sometimes pay off to stop and enjoy what you are seeing, rather than just marking off things you've seen on a checklist, like the Griswolds in *European Vacation*. Look, kids. Big Ben. Parliament.

If you've got the places listed you want to see, look for a pattern. Are they all close to a central location? If so, pick places where you can stay multiple nights and use them as bases of exploration around those regions.

Or can they be strung together in a circle over a larger region? If so, spend a couple nights in each place, moving around that circular route.

Be visual, pay attention to road maps, plan wisely, and try to avoid crisscrossing or backtracking. Check driving times between places with Via Michelin or Google Maps.

Then add about 25% to those driving times, as mapping programs don't take into account English roads. They twist and turn, which can keep speeds down lower than the actual posted speed limit. We were driving one road along the border of Scotland and England and ended up back in Scotland three times as we searched for Hadrian's Wall.

There are hills and valleys, sheep and cattle, tractors and tour buses, and even road works. You don't want to spend all of the time driving; trust me. It gets very tiring, especially as you will likely be driving a manual transmission, which are the majority rental cars available (automatics are available at a higher cost).

I try keeping my driving time to around three hours at the most and break it up with stops at attractions along the way.

I find the most reliable way to figure a distance and time is to multiply the miles by 35mph to get an average travel time. Example: If I need to travel fifty miles to my next accommodation, at the average speed limit of 35 mph, the drive alone will take approximately an hour-and-a-half.

Add onto this the time it takes to get to attractions, then add some additional time for stopping for lunch, photo opportunities, and exploring the side streets and quaint shops. What does that sign say? Let's see where it goes.

If you enlist in a travel agent to help you design an itinerary, be sure to ask about the agent's personal experience in England. It's quite common for agents to sell custom itineraries but actually never having visited England themselves and thus do not have any real experience. Be sure to work with a professional who specializes in English travel and has hands-on experience and knowledge as a local would.

Airfare

This is usually the biggest chunk of your travel budget. There is a definite season for vacationing in England, summer. While many people do go on the "peak" months of June, July and August, there is indeed a reason why summer is the best.

The days are much longer to see sights, warmer weather, less rain and wind, and everything is open. This also means the airfare is the most expensive, as well as hotels. Smaller accommodation, like B&Bs and guesthouses, have much the same rates year-round.

The shoulder months of March, April, and May, and September, October, and November are becoming more popular, as the weather is still usually decent, and the days aren't incredibly short yet.

However, this also means the airfares are creeping up as these become more popular times to travel. Please note some places won't be open in the shoulder and off seasons, many B&Bs, some restaurants, and most attractions may close after October and remain closed until mid-March.

If you are in doubt, check the attraction's website first to see if your "must-see" sights are open before making definitive plans. Most sites list daily opening hours, as well as their open season.

When I've decided on what I want to see and where I want to stay, I look for the most convenient airport(s), then I start researching my flights. I go to dozens of websites, sometimes daily, to watch fares before buying.

When I've flown to England, I found good fares on a one-day fare sale, which I only knew about due to a Fare Alert email I had signed up for. The fare was gone in an hour, but I'd pounced on it and got it. Do your research. There are deals out there, but you must train yourself to recognize the deal when you see it.

Also consider flying into one city and out of another. This is great for England, as you can fly into London, explore north and west, then fly out of Manchester at the end of your trip. This is called an open-jaw ticket, and usually doesn't cost much more, if any, than a normal round-trip ticket.

Also don't forget to check the airline websites; if you find a great fare on Expedia for Delta, Delta might have it cheaper on their own site, and it is usually better to deal directly rather than through a middleman. Some airlines, like Southwest (which isn't international, but could get you to a hub like New York cheaper) may not be listed on price consolidation sites like Travelocity, Kayak, or Expedia.

I sign up for airfare alerts when I'm researching fares, so I get quick notification of sales. Airfarewatchdog and Googleflights are great places to keep track of a particular fare, as the site follows airfare ups and downs.

You can set up email alerts for when the price rises or drops a particular amount or to a particular level. Some of the consolidation websites do this as well.

When you buy your tickets, be sure to read the cancelation policies. Usually, the cheaper the flight, the less flexible the changes allowed. Make sure you are going before you purchase non-refundable, no-change tickets.

If you have any reason why you might not be able to make the flight, either pay extra for flexible tickets, or get travel insurance that covers flight cancelation. Some fares cover delays or cancelations due to medical reasons, for instance.

Keep in mind they usually mean YOUR medical reason, not a child or a parent for whom you need to stay to take care of. Airlines are very strict about cancelations so be sure to read the fine print

before buying your tickets. And after COVID, any that had any coverage of pandemics removed them.

Accommodation

Bed & Breakfasts and Guesthouses

Once you have your airfare and itinerary, you know which nights you need accommodation and in which locations. England is wonderfully full of adorable bed & breakfasts; I highly recommend this accommodation choice.

The B&Bs in the United States tend to be more upscale and expensive than those in the England, so don't go by American examples. Most B&Bs I've ever been in have been comfortable, clean, cozy, and a delight to stay.

B&Bs around the countryside run around £40-50 per person sharing per night (pppn or pps) and include the traditional full English breakfast. You will pay more dearly for city locations or resort towns, especially during high season.

Where B&Bs are generally family homes, larger guesthouses are purpose-built B&Bs with higher occupation numbers, perhaps more amenities, and a more extensive breakfast menu, and will have a slightly higher cost.

If you are staying in the city, and have more than just a couple people, it may be more economical to rent a flat (an apartment). See the section on self-catering rentals below.

Hotels

Hotels usually charge by room rather than per person but are based on two people sharing. Many usually do not include breakfast in the deal, referred to on booking as "room only." Hotels are usually more cookie-cutter and sterile.

A Hilton is the same in San Francisco as it is in New York, London, and Japan, and they lack the authenticity of a family-run B&B. In my opinion, hotels are a place to stay based on convenience rather than a place to enjoy.

However, there are some small family-run hotels in rural areas which may offer you the privacy you want while also adding something interesting to your overall visit to England. Many old country houses have been converted to guesthouses and small hotels, which would definitely add interest to your stay in the region, especially if the accommodation has any historic ties to local history.

You can also find castle hotels around the country, such as Amberley Castle in West Sussex, or Hever Castle in Kent. You can even stay in Alnwick Castle, which was one of the inspirations for Hogwarts in the Harry Potter movies.

Prices in these types of accommodation are generally more expensive but would certainly add something special to your trip, especially if you're traveling to England for a special event, like an anniversary or honeymoon.

Hostels and Other Specialist Accommodation

Hostels (both regular hostels and youth hostels), camping, caravanning (RV), canal boats, colleges offering dormitory rooms for the summer, are other options for creative accommodation. There is no end of unusual places to stay. Some hostels in England are part of old castles, such as St. Briavels Castle Hostel in Gloucestershire. There are some churches and monasteries that are now B&Bs. Get creative.

Self-Catering

Self-catering houses are also an option, especially if you have a large group or prefer the privacy of a "home from home" type of accommodation. The biggest downfall is many require a seven-day minimum stay, usually from Saturday to Saturday. Some are willing to rent for short breaks, though, so always check.

Once you have decided where you want to stay, make a reservation. Make sure to check the cancelation policies with all accommodation you book. Most B&Bs and guesthouses require a 24- to 48-hour cancelation, and many hotels can be canceled the morning of arrival.

However, self-catering and specialty accommodation usually have a four-to-six-week cancelation period for a full refund. The time you cancel will dictate how much of your money you get back.

Inside that four-to-six-week period means staged refunds, with service charges increasing the closer to your reservation date.

Email is usually the normal option for communication these days. I prefer this method as it leaves a "paper trail," and I make sure to bring a copy with me.

Keep in mind that not everyone is web-savvy, even if they have a website, so be patient. Some may require a phone call, most will require a credit card to secure bookings, even if it's not charged. This protects the establishment against "no-shows."

Don't forget the time difference. England is ahead of Eastern Standard Time by five hours, and by eight hours from Pacific Standard Time. Noon in New York and 9 a.m. in San Francisco is 5 p.m. in England. If you're organizing your trip in the evening after work, remember the folks in England could be asleep.

Also, when booking your accommodation, not all places in England are going to take credit cards. Those which do may not take American Express or Discover.

Those which take credit cards will take Mastercard and Visa. Some are cash only, EVEN if they take a card number for the reservation. Be prepared to pay cash on departure, or make sure you've asked ahead of time.

If a host is going to take a deposit or take the full amount on booking, remember you will see a foreign transaction fee on your statement.

Ground Transportation

My recommendation for getting around England is definitely by renting a car, as discussed earlier. Exceptions would be if you are under or over the age limit for rentals, or maybe you have physical limitations. Also, if you're staying in a major city, like London or York. In places like that, you won't need a car because the city is compact enough to walk. Besides, parking is hard to find and expensive.

In the countryside, though, while it is possible to use buses and trains to get around, and certainly many people do, you won't find this an easy option, as it requires a lot of flexibility in your schedule. National Rail travels between cities and major towns, but a vast part of the country has no rail travel at all. Getting to villages and remote attractions can be difficult to impossible and very time-consuming.

If you are in an organized bus tour, you are obliged to stick to that itinerary, so you can't make a detour on a whim to go find a hidden castle when you see a sign. You can't stay longer at one spot unless you want to get left behind. There is no flexibility with organized tours.

If you travel by public bus, you do have some flexibility in your itinerary, but you will be reliant on the bus schedule, which is often inconsistent for arrival and departure times.

Now, I know it is scary to think about driving on the "wrong" side of the road, but it's not really that difficult, especially if you're a good, conscientious driver by nature. It's not so bad as you think, and you will get used to it very quickly. The mind has an incredible ability to "mirror" and allow you to perform the same tasks, as if mirroring the motions to what you're used to.

It helps to have a designated navigator, as the signage in England is a little different from what you may be used to. Signs might only list the name of the next town, or they may add the route number and the distance in miles to other towns on that route.

This means you should know the major towns on the way to where you are going, or even the ones just beyond your destination.

Most folks have map apps on their smartphones. If you don't have a data plan that you can use abroad, a GPS can still be very helpful. Not only does it help you find places, it helps you find your way back to your B&B. Keep in mind that any map tool is only good if you have a good address for the place. That's not always a given, especially in rural areas. I have made a habit of noting longitude and latitude for places I would be upset if I couldn't find.

Another consideration is data. If you have to pay a premium for international data rates, a GPS or a local sim card for your unlocked phone will be much less expensive than using your map app all day.

It can definitely help you find your way BACK to your B&B if you deliberately get lost during the day, just for the fun of it.

Big cities in England don't require a car to get around. In fact, having a car is a liability in London. It's difficult to get around with the heavy traffic, find parking is challenging unless you know where the few multi-story parking lots are, and it can be expensive both on the street and in the multi-story.

Also, London has fantastic public transportation systems, and the major attraction areas are highly walkable. Smaller towns and villages are very walkable as well, so parking for the afternoon and exploring the town by foot is usually the best option.

For other big cities, if it's your final stop before returning home, turn in the car before getting to the city, or wait to rent it until you leave to begin your holiday.

Gasoline is called petrol in England (gas is the natural stuff pumped into your home) and is very expensive. At the time of this publication, the cost is running around $7 USD per gallon. Yes, really.

The good news is you can usually get around 45 mpg from economy size cars (larger cars get slightly lower miles per gallon).

However, filling up a tank can still cost you $100 or more, so budget accordingly.

Remember the itinerary you made with estimated driving times? Use that mileage and double it. Yes, double it. You will be going to places, taking day trips, going out for dinner, stopping at brown sign sites, all sorts of side trips.

I've gotten decent deals from AutoEurope and from Enterprise Rental. I would advise against renting from a place you've never heard of. Cars can be very expensive, and if there's an issue, it's difficult to fight a fraudulent damage claim from overseas.

Having said that, there are a number of privately owned rental companies who have been in business as many as fifty years.

See more on the details and problems of renting a car above in the GROUND TRANSPORTATION section.

OTHER CONSIDERATIONS

Okay, you've done your research, gotten your airline tickets, made your reservations for accommodation, and your car rental. Ready to go? Not yet.

Travel Insurance

You break your leg the week before the trip. Ruined. All your money lost. Not so, Grasshopper, as long as you planned ahead and bought the proper travel insurance.

If you're booking with a travel agent (remember travel agents?), then they'll likely get insurance for your trip as a whole. However, you can still do this if you're self-planning. I use a handy comparison website called *Insure My Trip* and compare the benefits of different packages.

Find out if your own health insurance will cover you on foreign soil (some credit cards also have built-in travel insurance). Look for things like cancelation insurance in case of medical emergency, reimbursement for lost luggage, additions to the above-mentioned car insurance, etc.

Compare the benefits between what you already pay for and what you need to travel and find a travel plan which fits right for your needs. For a small investment, you get a great deal of peace of mind.

Keep in mind that in the past, some insurance has covered travel costs in case of a pandemic. Be VERY vigilant about checking for such language, as a lot of insurances got hit hard during COVID and have removed that coverage across the board. The language you're looking for is "trip cancelation coverage" that is valid for any reason.

Passports and Visas

For most people traveling to England, all they need is a valid passport from their country of origin. Some countries might also require some sort of travel visa, but that's not required for US or Canadian citizens.

Also, be sure there are no impediments that would cause refused entry, such as a felony record or outstanding warrants. This should be taken care of before you even buy your tickets.

Normal processing times for a new passport is six weeks, but please give it plenty of leeway (especially if you've already bought non-refundable tickets). This can increase to about twelve weeks without notice.

Don't procrastinate. My husband had mailed his application several months before, but while they cashed the check, they ended up losing the application. We only found out about that a few weeks before traveling, because we hadn't gotten a passport yet. We had to pay more for another application and expedited processing. Then, we ended up getting his passport the morning we flew out. We were very nervous, to say the least.

US citizens don't need visas for visits of up to ninety days in England, but if you are going somewhere else or staying longer, do read up on the requirements long before your flight, and make sure all paperwork is in order.

I mentioned earlier that travelers from the US don't require additional documents, but starting in January 2024, anyone traveling to one of 30 countries in Europe will require an ETIAS authorization. While England is not currently on that list, make sure that hasn't changed before you go, or if you plan on going to another country on the same trip.

Money

England uses the British Pound Sterling (£) for its currency. The exchange rate fluctuates every day, of course, but it tends to be somewhere between $1.00 and $1.40 per £1.

Cash

I recommend going to your bank and getting some Pounds as travel money for the day you land. You can always get more during your stay from the ATM, and/or use your credit card for purchases. The exchange rates through ATMs are usually on par with whatever you'd get elsewhere, though if your bank charges a high withdrawal fee, I'd minimize the number of transactions.

You can get some pre-trip sterling online through companies like AAA or Thomas Cooke or order it from your bank. I don't recommend getting a lot—just some emergency funds in case you're stuck somewhere without a working ATM.

Alternatively, larger airports have Bureau de Change desks where you can exchange your money for sterling. Keep in mind the exchange rate is higher in the airport for the convenience.

Travelers Checks

NEVER travel with large amounts of cash. Travelers checks were an option for many years, but now, you'd be hard-pressed to find anyplace that accepts or exchanges them. Just... don't.

ATMs in England

Be sure your bank is part of the LINK system to access your account in England. Also, you will not be given a choice between two accounts which are connected in your bank. Your ATM card will only have access to your primary account from England, which is often your checking account.

You may wish to save hassle while in England by opening a dedicated travel account and getting a new ATM card for that one, and make sure any and all travel funds you wish to access are there.

Also, keep in mind that smaller towns and villages might not have an ATM. You may have to travel to a larger town nearby to get cash. I've also noticed some ATMs (often, the only one in town) are inside stores, so if the store is closed, so is access to cash.

However, as more gas stations open which are parts of small convenience shops, small ATMs in the back of the shops are often installed. Plan accordingly if you're traveling to a remote area, and keep in mind that banks are usually open from 9 a.m. - 4 p.m. weekdays, and in the remotest areas, may have sparse hours.

Credit Cards

Be sure to contact your bank prior to travel, to let them know to expect charges made in England during your travel dates. This will, hopefully, save you the hassle of having your card put on hold, or worse, canceled, mid-trip and leaving you without your card.

Many cards have a "travel authorization" on the website, where you can enter country and dates of travel. Sometimes their fraud department will still put a hold on, but a phone call can often clear this up. Make sure that you have that phone number handy if it's not printed on the card itself.

If you don't have a credit card, or your interest rate is too high, shop around for a card with a good rate. Many (Capital One is one of the few which don't) add on an extra 2% for any foreign transaction, in addition to the 1% Visa/MC charges.

You don't want to carry too much cash with you. However, some B&Bs, while preferring cash even if they take credit cards, require reservations made guaranteeing the booking with a credit card to protect them against "no-shows."

You could also set up a prepaid debit card that is based on sterling and use it throughout the trip, including getting cash from the ATM. I've heard of some issues with American credit cards that use six-digit PINs in the UK which only uses four digits. Be sure your card uses a four-digit PIN and avoid those problems.

Many places in the UK (including England) have now changed over to a chip and pin format for all credit cards and laser/ATM cards. While the machine in most shops takes both chip and pin and swipe cards, shop staff may not have been trained how to use the swiper or how to manually enter the card number. You may need to ask for a manager to complete your charge.

Packing

Sure, you've packed dozens of times for vacations. What's the big deal? Well, the flight luggage restrictions for carry-on and checked luggage, for one. Airlines have lots of rules, so it behooves you to know them before you get to the airport.

Carry-on: Most airlines have their carry-on rules on their websites. Some have weight as well as size restrictions. Airlines differ, but you may find your carry-on must fit under the seat in front of you, even if you intend on putting it in the overhead compartment, and it must not weigh more than around fifteen to twenty pounds.

Liquid restrictions also need to be obeyed. Check before you go. Right now, any carry-on liquids must be in containers no larger than 3oz (100ml) and they must all fit comfortably in a quart-sized clear Ziploc bag. Liquids include gels and semi-solid things roll-on deodorant and toothpaste, so do be careful. When in doubt and you absolutely don't need it for your flight, check it in your luggage or leave it at home.

Jackets and medical equipment (like CPAP machines) are not counted toward your carry-on limits, though cameras and laptop computers are. I've taken heavy things from my carry-on and put them in my purse, which is rarely weighed.

You can also stuff the pockets of the jacket. I packed some of my heavy electronic stuff, like chargers and batteries, into my CPAP machine case.

It's highly recommended you carry prescriptions with you rather than putting them in your checked luggage. In the event your luggage gets misdirected, you will still have your medication. Prescription medicines must be labeled in the traveler's name. Be sure to get your doctor to write out a copy of your prescription and carry it with you in a safe place. If you lose your medication, bring your prescription to a chemist to have refilled.

If you're carrying baby food or formula, it may need to be tested at the gate. Where adult food is concerned, you will be asked at security to dispose of things like uneaten food, and open bottles and cans of water or colas. Visit the Transport Security Administration (TSA) website for lists of acceptable carry-ons and restrictions. This list will also help you to know what you can bring on board to entertain yourself or your kids, such as electronic games, music players, laptops, tablets, eReaders, etc.

The site will also provide you with information on things like knitting needles, crochet hooks, scissors, etc. Keep in mind that even if it's on the TSA acceptance list, it's purely up to the discretion of the officers at security. Don't bring your expensive needles and hooks in the event they're not allowed, and you have to throw them away.

Checked luggage: Some airlines charge hefty fees for overweight luggage and limit the number of pieces each person can check. While airline restrictions vary, for long-haul flights into the UK, the maximum weight allowance is usually about fifty pounds, and some airlines can allow up to two fifty-pound suitcases per person.

Also, if you're in the habit of locking your suitcases, be sure to use TSA approved locks. If inspectors need to access your suitcases for any reason, they have a master key to open those locks, or they will cut off non-TSA locks to inspect. If there is an inspection, you'll know when you get home to unpack and find an inspection notice on top of your items. TSA approved locks are available in most travel sections in department stores and travel shops, as well as stores like Target, WalMart, etc.

Don't, don't, don't put valuables or medicines in your checked luggage. I cannot emphasize this enough, yet people do it every day. Cameras, laptops, anything fragile, anything essential, must go in your carry-on. There's even a reality show based on people buying up abandoned and lost luggage, hoping for hidden treasure inside.

Of course, this makes your carry-on heavy, so some decision-making is sometimes necessary, as you've seen above, there are strict weight limits for carry-ons.

I usually put one day's worth of clean clothes in my carry-on, in case the checked luggage is delayed or lost, as well as electronics, meds, and travel documents.

If you have something really valuable, consider leaving it at home. Do you really need the diamond stud earrings on the trip, or will the cubic zirconia work?

My last trip, I did carry-on only for the sixteen-day trip. My luggage was delayed too many times in the past. On my last trip to Scotland, my baggage was delayed for five days. Luckily, I had a change of clothes and most of my required paperwork, so it was okay, even if annoying.

Bring a soft-sided carry-on or luggage, as it will likely expand with the things you buy on your trip. Some are expandable with zippered sides.

Or just bring an extra duffel bag to check on the way back. It's much less annoying to wait five days for your dirty clothes to arrive home than it is for your clean clothes to arrive on vacation.

Jet Lag

The bane of travelers. Many people suffer from jet lag when they travel across time zones. If you are in the eastern US, you will be five hours ahead in England. If you are from the western US, that increased to eight hours.

While everyone's body reacts differently, here are some tips that I've followed or heard in the past that might help.

- **Hydrate:** drink plenty of water during your flights. This helps keep your body functioning normally and reduces travel stress. Drinking alcohol can make the problem worse, so go easy on the cocktails, as they can dehydrate you.
- **Sleep:** if you can sleep on the overnight trip, do so. Even if it is only a couple of hours, this will help. I usually use earplugs and eyeshades to block noise and light. I try not to sleep very much the night before the flight, so I sleep better on the plane. Your mileage may vary.
- **Routine:** I tend to go to bed an hour earlier for each of the three days before my trip. For instance, if I normally go to bed at 10pm, I will go at 9 p.m. three days before my flight, 8 p.m. two days before, 7 p.m. the night before, waking earlier each morning until the day of departure. That way, your body is a little more acclimatized to your new schedule, resulting in a smaller jolt once you arrive.
- **Activity:** When you do wake up, make sure to try to get some sunshine first thing. This wakes up your body and lets your circadian rhythm settle in. The day I arrive, I usually make sure to do things all day, and try to avoid napping (occasionally I give in, but make sure it's only an hour or two). I don't plan anything heavy, like a two-hour drive or climbing a mountain.

Light activity, some sightseeing, walking around the town. Then I usually crash around 9pm, and sleep like the dead. The next morning, I'm bright-eyed and bushy-tailed, ready to tackle the world. Getting into your normal sleep pattern right away helps. Wake at your normal time and go to bed at your normal time. Even on arrival day.

- **Sugar levels:** Invariably, my husband has a sugar crash halfway through the second day of the trip. We keep regular mealtimes and top up with power bars to counter any problems. Your body goes through a lot of stress through travel, especially if you are older or have muscular/metabolic issues, such as diabetes or fibromyalgia. Plan accordingly and make sure you have supplies on hand to combat them.

READY TO GO? Don't forget the smile.

Don't forget to pack the most important thing for any trip, a great attitude. This small item can make the worst disaster into a hilarious story and get you through a difficult situation with authorities and can take the biggest lemon and make lemonade out of it. After all, how can it be terrible, you're in England.

A trip to England will be full of wonderful memories, historic experiences, and meeting wonderful folks. Whether you get addicted like I have or are happy with going once and treasuring the memory forever, you will have an exquisite time.

Bolton Abbey, Skipton

DISCOUNTS AND DEALS

Make no mistake, budgeting is difficult. When you're planning a trip anywhere, one of the first things you do is look at your budget for the trip. Sometimes this can be intimidating, and you are left trying to figure out how to get the most out of your limited funds and resources. This section is designed to help you find ways to stretch those resources and get the best vacation your money can buy.

A lot of this will depend on when you go and how long you are going to stay. A week in January is going to be much less expensive than a week in August, especially if you are staying in London.

Airfare will be higher during the peak season of June, July and August. Then, it gets a bit lower on the shoulder seasons (March, April, and May, and September, October, and November). The lowest will be during the winter months, except around Christmas.

While it doesn't vary as capriciously, higher-end accommodations will also vary based on season. Some may even be closed during the winter months, so be warned and plan ahead.

The most important aspect of finding the best deal is RESEARCH. You must spend some time finding the deals and know enough to realize it's a good deal before buying. This applies to airfare, car rental, accommodation, entrance fees, train tickets… whatever you're looking for. What is a good deal? Like anything, it depends on what you're willing to pay versus how much you really want it. But I can give you some guidelines via my past experiences.

Planning

I start out with a list of the sites I most want to see and plot them out in a circle on the map, if I can. Then I research the areas around those places, to find the hidden places that most people don't visit.

That being said, the touristy spots are usually that way for a reason. A person can spend months in London and still not see all the things they want to see.

However, months of travel (even weeks of travel) can get expensive, especially when lots of places have admission fees.

There are several discount cards that can help reduce the cost of entering many monuments and properties. Many museums are actually free, by the way. Take advantage of that. English Heritage offers an Overseas Visitor Pass, as well as a Great British Heritage Pass. London City Cards for a variety of categories, BritRail Pass, Go City London Explorer Pass, York City Pass, Liverpool Pass, all offer discounted entry into many of England's historic attractions.

Do some research. If you plan on visiting five or more of the sites they cover, it may be well worth the cost. Not all historic sites are covered, so do look them up.

I find a great way to get a good overview of cities like London or York, and to travel around the cities, is to get tickets for the hop-on/hop-off bus which winds through the streets, stopping at various attractions and offering commentary. Look for the open-top buses. Hint: the enclosed buses are usually for local city travel, not tourists.

You usually don't need to pre-book these tours. Just show up at one of the stops, which are signposted around the city. Your ticket is good for twenty-four hours, so if you get on the bus at 1 p.m. (the last tour out is a pick-up tour at 5 p.m.), you can get back on the bus first thing in the morning for free. You can then continue sightseeing until 1pm, though they may allow you back on the rest of the day, if you get a nice driver.

I have enjoyed the hop-on/hop-off bus in many major cities, including London, Edinburgh, Dublin, New York City, Toronto,

San Francisco, Chicago, and Washington DC, and always find it entertaining and useful.

Also, I recommend the live commentary buses, as the canned ones tend to be less lively and lack humor. Each time I've gone, I manage to get a host who sings for us, not necessarily very well, but with great enthusiasm.

Airfare

Usually, direct flights are less expensive, but that isn't always the case. However, they are less likely to mislay your luggage during a layover.

Sometimes flying into or from a major hub, such as Newark or London, can help keep the costs down. Sometimes it's the only viable option. For instance, there are no direct flights from my closest airport to England, so I always have to fly to a larger airport that handles jets. The last trip, I had to fly from New Haven to Boston, to London. Check out the planning section for airfare for more information.

I use several tools for airfare research. Kayak is a strong tool, as is Googleflights. There are others, but keep in mind that for any consolidator (like Kayak), that's one more layer of administration to wade through if something goes wrong.

I research on the consolidators, but often then go to the airline site itself. If I can find the exact flights at the same or similar price, I buy them there. If the flight is delayed or canceled, you are more likely to get better service in fixing it if you book direct.

I also sign up for email alerts from the airlines I might use, such as Delta or American. If you get notification of a great sale, and you know you are going, jump on it right away. That deal may be sold out in an hour.

Also, I prefer to have control of my travel times. Some airlines consider a 45-minute layover to be "legal," but that makes me way too anxious, in case of a delayed flight. I prefer two hours, minimum, especially for international flights. Anything less and your luggage may not arrive when you do. It's up to your personal level of comfort for chaos how you book your tickets.

If you're a student or a veteran, there are websites, such as Student Universe or Veterans Advantage which can help you with better airfare.

Having enough frequent flyer miles with a particular airline (many credit cards allow you to accumulate these) can also either defray or replace the costs of a flight overseas. However, keep in mind many might have blackout periods, and sometimes seats are more difficult to get if you are using miles to obtain them. Some airlines allow you to apply your miles to a portion of the cost, reducing the total, no matter what the seat or flight.

Transportation

Renting a car is, by far, my highest recommended mode of transportation when traveling in England. However simple this may sound, it's fraught with peril and complexity, hidden charges and downright fraud. Please see my GROUND TRANSPORTATION advice in the previous section for lots of details on how to avoid, or at least minimize, them.

Another option is train travel. A Britrail pass may be helpful. However, the trains aren't quite as all-encompassing as traveling by car, and once you get to those hubs, you must find another way to travel around the enchanting countryside. Britrail travels between the cities and large towns but will not get you to the smaller destinations.

There are several other options. You could base yourself in that town or village and take daily private tours or a larger organized coach tour, or rent a horse-drawn caravan, cycle or hike. You could hire a camper (caravan) and sleep in that instead of a B&B or hotel. Or just visit the town or village in a more relaxed local kind of way. It's all up to your style of travel, your budget, desires, and sometimes your physical limitations.

Accommodation

While I'm in England, I greatly prefer staying at Bed & Breakfasts as my accommodation choice. However, sometimes hotels are a better choice, such as the night before flying out of the airport, or in London, where B&Bs aren't as prevalent.

B&Bs can average £35-50 per person sharing per night (pppn) and include the famous traditional Full English Breakfast. Specialty B&Bs (historic houses, castle B&Bs, etc.) are usually a bit more expensive.

I prefer B&Bs but occasionally splurge for a charming, historically significant place, or the odd thatched cottage. Keep in mind this is per person per night, and therefore, twice as much for two people in the one room.

Single rooms are slightly higher, averaging £40-45. Some B&Bs have family rooms at a discounted rate per person, perhaps £35 pppn. Again, it depends on your personal level of comfort and sharing with your traveling companions. I have more information on accommodation in the previous section.

If you really want to splurge, you can always spend some time in a castle. Yes, you can find smaller castle accommodations than the five-star hotels. They are few but include some B&B accommodation and self-catering, and there's even a castle hostel.

However, if you have your heart set on a castle stay, keep in mind lots of hotels have "castle" in their names, but aren't necessarily in an actual castle. Do some research on their website, first.

What's the cheapest accommodation while traveling in England? Camping out, of course. It's not my cup of tea, but plenty of people do it, especially if they have a bike or are hiking the countryside. You could also stay at hostels for a great discounted stay.

Youth hostels are no longer separate from other hostels, today's difference being average hostels and specialty hostels. In other words, age is no longer a defining factor to using a hostel. Typical hostels are purpose-built accommodation with shared dorms with shared bathrooms. English Youth Hostels Association (YHA) is a popular site for booking around the country.

Another option, particularly good if you've a large group, is a self-catering house. These are usually standalone houses or cottages, with a varying amount of space, for rent in usually week-long periods, most often from Saturday to Saturday. Occasionally, usually off high season, you can get "short breaks" of two to three days instead.

Sometimes this is an option in the city, as well. We rented a two-story flat in Leeds, complete with brick arched ceilings. It had a vaulted ceiling in the dining room, 2 bedrooms downstairs, and a small one-bedroom flat above it (they could be rented out separately).

There are several places to find self-catering lodges, but I recommend going through a well-known agent, such as VRBO, Booking.com, Cottages.com, or VisitEngland. And, of course, you can explore the AirB&B options wherever you travel.

Food

Food can be an expensive part of your trip, or a very cheap one, depending on your planning and habits. Staying at a B&B can be a big part of this, the enormous breakfast your hosts provide will keep you fueled into the afternoon or early evening, if you let it.

We often do this, and then grab a pub meal late in the day for about £10 per person. Then we may have a light supper at another pub or have takeaway.

Sometimes, if we're out hiking or exploring, we just grab snack foods at the local grocery store to bring with us instead of stopping for lunch. Bread, cheese and smoked salmon are delicious local options and are great in sandwiches made on the go.

I did this a lot on a November trip, as I was jealous of my scarce daylight sightseeing time. I packed snacks to munch on during the day, and only had an inside meal at breakfast and dinner.

Often, we've grown hungry mid-afternoon, only to find that many full-service restaurants are closed at that time. Some close after 2 p.m. and don't reopen until 4 or 5 p.m. for dinner, so plan accordingly. Some pubs will still serve food during that time and takeaways are often open as well.

Late night dining (after 8 p.m.) has a similar problem, with the same solutions. I remember one night, having landed in London and then rented a car, driving north to a town near Nottingham. By the time we arrived, it was just after 8pm. The small town had only a few pubs, and none were serving food that late. After searching five more places, we ended up two towns over and had a delightful supper with the pub quiz crowd.

If you're staying at a self-catering house, you will have a kitchen where you can prepare meals at home rather than paying for expensive meals at restaurants. Granted, you are then not offered your Full English Breakfast from the B&B, but sometimes all you want is a bowl of cereal or some toast when you wake up.

Some privately owned self-catering house owners will supply, at no extra cost, fresh eggs for your fridge (especially if they have their own chickens), or even the makings for a Full English Breakfast for the length of your stay.

Drink

Pints are larger in England than in the US, so drink carefully. And a half-pint of beer or cider is about the same price as the same amount of soda, so enjoy your drink.

Don't dare drink and drive, though. The penalties for such are high, and those roads are scary enough while you are sober. While you won't get points on your home driver's license, you may get arrested and the car impounded, which results in many costs, as well as a call to the embassy.

If you don't wish to pay the pub price, you can always go to the off license (liquor store), purchase some pints, and take them to the B&B to enjoy. Of course, then you miss out on the pub culture.

Things To Do

In addition to the many places already discussed above, numerous galleries and museums in England are free of charge, a great way to spend a day, especially if the weather isn't great.

On finer days, many parks and gardens are free as well. You often can find local festivals and fairs to shop in, listen to music, sample food, and have a grand time with little to no cost. Of course, the landscapes are free to view, as are many historical landmarks.

Children

Sometimes it is very difficult to plan trips when you have children. Whether your kids are young children or rebellious teenagers, finding places which have enough to keep them interested and engaged can be quite a challenge.

There's an excellent resource I discovered called Travel for Kids, which has sections for many places, including England. Lots of museums and exhibits include interactive stuff for kids to enjoy, so keep an eye out for those. A day full of seeing ruined abbey after ruined castle after ruined abbey is enough to bore even many adults, much less children. And having cranky children does not help anyone enjoy their vacation.

Wi-Fi

Most hotels and many B&Bs have now started offering free Wi-Fi, though it's not always GOOD Wi-Fi, and some turn it off during the night hours. Many cafès have it, though, as will any McDonalds (not that I recommend going to McDonalds when you have so many other great options).

Libraries will also have access. Some entire cities now offer free Wi-Fi, so do some research ahead of time to plan. There are apps to help you find Wi-Fi spots wherever you are.

Summary

Remember earlier when I said a trip to England was less expensive than a trip to Disney? Our last trip to England, which was two weeks in August, was about $4,000 for airfare, rental car, trip insurance, B&Bs, and food. You could spend more than this on two weeks in New York City, or at Disney. And there are all sorts of ways you can trim your budget even more on your trip.

HIDDEN GEMS

There is not enough room to include all the fantastic places to visit in England. However, there are loads of books which concentrate on popular sites. While I'll mention some of those, I will be concentrating on the hidden gems, those places off the beaten path that might not be in the other travel guides.

I've broken the country into nine geographical regions, and then further by County within those regions.

NORTHEAST

Northumberland

Hadrian's Wall: An iconic landmark, Hadrian's Wall stands as a testament to the Roman Empire's ancient might. Stretching 73 miles from the banks of the River Tyne to the Solway Firth, it offers breathtaking vistas of the English countryside. Wander along its lengths and imagine Roman soldiers keeping an eye out for Picts from the north.

Alnwick Castle: Recognize this majestic castle from somewhere? Maybe from "Harry Potter" as Hogwarts? Alnwick Castle is one of the largest inhabited castles in England and, aside from its movie stardom, it has a rich history dating back nearly a thousand years. While here, don't miss Alnwick Garden with its notorious Poison Garden.

Lindisfarne (Holy Island): Cut off twice a day by tides, Lindisfarne is a tidal island with an enchanting aura. Its historic monastery was the heart of Christianity in Anglo-Saxon times, and the island is soaked in spiritual ambiance. Remember to check the tide tables before visiting; you wouldn't want to get stranded (or perhaps you would?).

Cragside House, Gardens and Estate: This estate was the first house in the world to be lit by hydroelectricity. The sprawling estate boasts beautiful gardens, one of the largest rock gardens in Europe, and an intricate network of footpaths. Sir William Armstrong, Victorian inventor and landscape genius, was the brain behind this wonder.

Barter Books: In the heart of Alnwick, this second-hand bookshop is located in an old railway station. If you're a book lover, prepare to lose hours here. With roaring fires in winter, comfy sofas, and the allure of forgotten literary gems, this place is sheer magic.

St Cuthbert's Cave: This is a hidden chamber in the woods where, legend has it, the monks of Lindisfarne hid St Cuthbert's body from Viking raiders. The tranquility of this place, surrounded by dense woodlands and the whispers of ancient tales, truly gives it an otherworldly feel.

Roughting Linn Waterfall: This is a secluded waterfall surrounded by a tranquil woodland setting. The area also features ancient rock art, believed to date back to the Bronze Age. The peaceful surroundings and the sense of mystery make this a delightful spot for visitors looking for something off the beaten path.

Tyne and Wear

Baltic Centre for Contemporary Art: Overlooking the River Tyne in Gateshead, this striking modern art haven is housed in a former flour mill. Baltic is the largest institution of its kind in the world, offering ever-changing exhibitions of contemporary art. Not just for art aficionados, the view of the Newcastle skyline from its viewing platform is breathtaking.

The Angel of the North: While driving in Gateshead, you'd be hard-pressed to miss Antony Gormley's majestic and iconic steel statue, which spreads its wings 54 meters across. Standing as a beacon of hope and a symbol of the North, this modern marvel never ceases to impress.

Tynemouth Priory and Castle: Positioned dramatically on a rocky headland overlooking the North Sea, this site has witnessed a rich tapestry of history. The ruins of the priory, dominated by its early Gothic chapel, create an aura of enchantment. It's easy to imagine the lives of those from centuries past as the waves crash below.

Victoria Tunnel: This preserved 19th-century waggonway runs under the city from the Town Moor to the Tyne. Originally built to transport coal, it was used as an air-raid shelter during WWII. The guided tours here offer an eerie yet captivating journey through Newcastle's underbelly.

Saltwell Park: Tucked away in Gateshead is this Victorian gem, a delightful mix of woodland, ornamental gardens, and leisure facilities. The crowning jewel? Saltwell Towers, a fairytale-like mansion nestled at its heart. It's an oasis of calm and a perfect spot for a leisurely afternoon.

The Cathedral Church of St. Nicholas: For our touch of the mystical, head to this 15th-century cathedral in Newcastle. With its stained-glass windows casting ethereal glows, and legends of ghostly apparitions, there's an air of the mystical that surrounds this sacred space. Its Lantern Tower was once a beacon for ships on the River Tyne, guiding them safely to the port.

Durham

Durham Cathedral: Can't start a Durham list without mentioning this World Heritage site. Towering over the city, it's an architectural marvel. Whether you're a history buff, architecture enthusiast, or just someone looking for a bit of serenity, this cathedral won't disappoint. Its rib-vaulted ceilings and Norman architecture are downright awe-inspiring.

Durham Castle: Right next to the cathedral, this Norman castle is steeped in history. Once the residence of the Bishops of Durham, it's now a part of Durham University. Imagine studying where knights once roamed.

Crook Hall and Gardens: This Grade I listed medieval manor house is surrounded by a series of delightful gardens – including a Shakespearean garden, where you half expect to stumble upon a soliloquy in progress. With its maze, moat, and secret garden, it's a delightful escape from the bustle.

Finchale Priory: Located on the outskirts of Durham, these picturesque ruins by the River Wear tell tales of times gone by. Once a 13th-century Benedictine priory, the tranquility of its setting makes it a peaceful spot for reflection.

Oriental Museum: This is the only museum in the North of England solely dedicated to the art and archeology of the Orient. From ancient Egyptian mummies to Chinese porcelain, it's a trove of treasures waiting to be explored.

NORTHWEST

Cumbria

Lake Windermere: No visit to Cumbria is complete without seeing its most famous lake. Whether you fancy hopping on a steamboat, dipping your toes, or simply sitting by its edge with a picnic, Windermere is the place to be. And the surrounding town of Bowness-on-Windermere is as charming as they come.

Hadrian's Wall: Stepping back into Roman Britain, this formidable fortification stretches across the county. The remains are a testament to the might and reach of the Roman Empire. As you walk alongside, you can't help but ponder the legions that once patrolled here.

The Rum Story, Whitehaven: Located in Whitehaven's old Georgian Quarter, this attraction transports you into the world of the rum trade. It's interactive, atmospheric, and believe it or not, set in the original shop, courtyards, cellars, and bonded warehouses of the Jefferson family – once a major player in the rum world.

Long Meg and Her Daughters: Our mystical stop. This is one of the largest stone circles in the country and steeped in legend. Some say the stones are a coven of witches turned to stone by a wizard. As you walk amongst them, there's an undeniable aura of magic. Just be wary of any spell-casting while you're there.

St Bees Lighthouse: Perched on St Bees Head, this operational lighthouse offers spectacular views of the coastline and the Irish Sea. It's off the typical tourist track, making it an idyllic spot for those in search of some peace and picturesque vistas.

Aira Force Waterfall: Hidden near Ullswater in the Lake District, this magnificent waterfall is surrounded by lush woodland and flora. Following the meandering trails leading to the falls, especially after a rain, feels like stepping into a fairy tale.

Castlerigg Stone Circle: This is one of the most visually impressive prehistoric monuments in Britain and is among the earliest British circles, raised in about 3000 BCE during the Neolithic period. Its purpose remains a mystery, but many believe it had a religious or astronomical significance. Set against a backdrop of mountains, it's a spiritual place where visitors often feel a deep connection to the landscape and the ancients who once stood there.

Eskdale Mill: This is one of the oldest water-powered corn mills in England and stands as a testament to Cumbria's industrial heritage. Located in the picturesque Eskdale Valley, visitors can learn about traditional milling methods, explore the beautifully preserved machinery, and enjoy the tranquil surroundings.

Lancashire

Lancaster Castle: This historic fortress has seen over a thousand years of history. From the trials of the Pendle witches to tales of royalty and intrigue, it's a living testament to England's past. The guided tours here are an absolute treat.

Blackpool Tower and Promenade: An iconic British seaside escape. Whether you're braving the heights of the Tower, dancing in its grand ballroom, or simply enjoying the traditional Pleasure Beach attractions, Blackpool promises nostalgic fun.

Samlesbury Hall: This historic house, dating back to 1325, is brimming with tales of witches, spirits, and the rich tapestry of Lancashire life. Plus, its gardens are an absolute delight, and the hall often hosts events that bring its history to vibrant life.

Beacon Fell Country Park: A lush escape for nature lovers. This sprawling park offers beautiful woodland walks, picturesque vistas, and a variety of wildlife. It's a breath of fresh Lancashire air and a fantastic spot for picnics.

Clitheroe Castle: This ancient Norman castle has dominated the Ribble Valley skyline for over 800 years. While the castle itself is steeped in history, the local legends and folklore add an aura of mystery. Some say its grounds are haunted, others speak of age-old treasures. Either way, it's a place where the lines between history and myth blur beautifully.

The Tolkien Trail: For the fans of Middle-Earth, this lesser-known gem is a must. It's said that J. R. R. Tolkien was inspired by the Lancashire landscape when writing parts of his legendary series. This trail takes you through some of those stunning locales. Imagine, walking in the footsteps of hobbits.

Pendle Hill: This is both a natural and mystical site. Rising 557 meters above sea level, Pendle Hill is famous for its associations with the 17th century Pendle witch trials. Local legends and tales of witchcraft, along with the hill's looming presence, add to its mysterious aura. A hike to the summit offers panoramic views of the Lancashire countryside.

Greater Manchester

Manchester Cathedral: Nestled in the heart of the city, this medieval marvel boasts stunning Gothic architecture. With its intricate stained-glass windows and centuries-old choir stalls, it's a peaceful retreat amidst the city buzz. And if walls could talk, oh, the tales they'd tell.

The Museum of Science and Industry: Housed in the old railway station, this is a must-visit for curious minds. Dive into Manchester's rich industrial past, see the world's first stored-program computer, and explore historic aircraft and locomotives. It's a trip back in time, with a dash of futuristic wonder.

Chetham's Library: A hidden gem for sure. Established in 1653, it's the oldest free public reference library in the UK. Its oak-paneled reading room has witnessed the musings of many, including Marx and Engels. If you listen closely, you might hear whispers of revolutionary ideas in the air.

Afflecks: Embrace the quirky. This indie emporium in the Northern Quarter is a labyrinth of boutiques, tattoo parlors, and vinyl stores. Whether you're hunting for vintage fashion or niche artwork, this place is a treasure trove of Manchester's eclectic spirit.

Fletcher Moss Botanical Garden: In the suburb of Didsbury, you'll find this enchanting haven. With its rockeries, water features, and rare plants, it feels like a scene out of a fantasy novel. Our dash of the mystical for you.

St Mary's Roman Catholic Church: Located on Mulberry Street, this is the oldest post-Reformation Catholic church in Manchester. Inside, you're greeted by stunning artworks, delicate stonework, and a serene aura that feels worlds away from the bustling city.

Ordsall Hall: A historic manor house with parts dating back over 800 years, Ordsall Hall is steeped in history and legend. It's reputed to be one of Greater Manchester's most haunted places, with numerous ghost sightings and supernatural occurrences reported over the years.

Manchester's Hidden Tunnels: Under the city streets lie a series of tunnels, air-raid shelters, and subterranean passageways. Some of these can be explored through guided tours, offering a unique underground perspective on the city's history.

Merseyside

The Beatles Story, Liverpool: The Beatles' hometown offers this immersive museum. Dive deep into the life and times of the Fab Four, tracing their journey from the streets of Liverpool to global stardom. And maybe, just maybe, you'll leave with a song in your heart.

Merseyside Maritime Museum: An ode to the region's rich seafaring heritage. From tales of the Titanic to the maritime role in World War II, there's a vast ocean of history to uncover. Ahoy.

Birkenhead Park: Did you know that this park was an inspiration for New York's Central Park? It's a verdant oasis with picturesque bridges, boating lakes, and beautiful Victorian architecture. A perfect spot for that afternoon stroll.

Williamson's Tunnels: Delve beneath the streets of Liverpool to uncover this intricate network of tunnels. Mysteriously commissioned by the 19th-century philanthropist Joseph Williamson, their purpose remains a subject of speculation. A subterranean wonder, if ever there was one.

The Black Pearl, New Brighton: This driftwood pirate ship, nestled on the sands of New Brighton beach, looks like it's sailed straight out of a storybook. While it's not actually ancient, the charm, artistry, and the stories spun around it certainly lend an enchanting aura.

Port Sunlight Village: Created by Lord Leverhulme for his soap factory workers, this model village is a living testament to Victorian architecture and urban planning. The quaint cottages, lush gardens, and the Lady Lever Art Gallery, housing a world-class collection of art, make this more than just a trip – it's a step back in time.

Bidston Hill: Located on the Wirral Peninsula, Bidston Hill is home to ancient rock carvings, a historic windmill, and the Bidston

Observatory. Local legends speak of ghosts, witches, and other supernatural occurrences, making it a site of both historical and mystical intrigue.

Cheshire

Chester Roman Walls and Amphitheatre: When in Cheshire, you've got to step back into Roman times. The ancient city of Chester boasts the most complete Roman walls in Britain. Wander atop them, imagining the legions that once patrolled. And don't miss the Amphitheatre—Britain's largest. Gladiators, anyone?

Tatton Park: A sprawling estate that's a tapestry of lush gardens, deer parks, and the grand Tatton Hall. Whether you're rowing on the meres, wandering through the Japanese gardens, or indulging in a bit of history inside the mansion, there's a slice of Cheshire charm for everyone here.

Jodrell Bank Discovery Centre: Home to the mighty Lovell Telescope, this observatory lets you delve deep into the mysteries of the universe. It's not every day you stand beneath one of the world's leading radio telescopes, right?

Little Moreton Hall: This place is straight out of a storybook. This Tudor half-timbered manor seems to defy gravity with its crooked architecture. Wandering its rooms is like stepping into a whimsical dream—or perhaps down a rabbit hole?

Whitegate Way: This old railway line turned nature trail is a peaceful retreat. Meandering through woodlands, wetlands, and meadows, it's a slice of Cheshire's tranquil countryside. And, if you're lucky, you might stumble upon some of its more secretive inhabitants, like the kingfisher or water vole.

Chester Cathedral: An architectural masterpiece with a history stretching back over 1,000 years, the cathedral boasts beautiful Gothic and Romanesque features. Its ancient monastic cloisters, medieval carvings, and vibrant stained-glass windows are particularly noteworthy.

Alderley Edge: This sandstone ridge offers panoramic views of the Cheshire Plain. It's also steeped in myth and legend, with tales of wizards, magical horses, and hidden treasures. The most famous legend tells of a wizard who puts a troop of sleeping knights and their white horses under a spell, waiting to be awakened in Britain's hour of need. Be sure to seek The Wizard Inn.

YORKSHIRE

South Yorkshire

Magna Science Adventure Centre: Housed in a former steelworks, this science adventure park is a blend of industrial history and hands-on exploration. Feel the heat of fire tornadoes, witness water-based antics, and maybe even dance in the rain. It's the alchemy of the elements in all its glory.

Sheffield Botanical Gardens: A sprawling green haven in the heart of Sheffield, these gardens are a serene retreat with a dash of

Victorian elegance. The glass pavilions, landscaped hills, and rare plants transport you to another era, and perhaps even another world.

Wentworth Woodhouse: This majestic mansion has the widest façade of any stately home in Europe. Steeped in history and surrounded by gardens and parkland, it's an architectural wonder waiting to share its stories.

Kelham Island Museum: Dive deep into Sheffield's steelmaking history at this industrial museum. It's not just about relics, though. The River Don Engine, a massive steam engine, is still in working order and is an absolute treat when in action.

Brodsworth Hall and Gardens: This Victorian country house is a slice of history frozen in time. But it's the gardens, with their fairy tale topiaries, whispering fountains, and secret corners, that add a touch of magic. Rumor has it, the statues come alive at night.

Conisbrough Castle: This Norman castle boasts a unique circular keep, offering panoramic views of the region. Its storied past is filled with tales of kings, wars, and sieges. As you wander its ruins, there's an air of ancient mystery that clings to every stone.

West Yorkshire

The Cragg Vale Coiners: In the heart of the Pennines, Cragg Vale was once home to a notorious group of counterfeit coin makers in the 18th century. The myth and legend surrounding their deeds have become part of local folklore. The atmospheric landscape of Cragg Vale adds to the mysterious allure of these tales.

Saltaire Village: Founded by Sir Titus Salt, a leading industrialist in the wool industry, Saltaire is a well-preserved Victorian-era model village. Recognized as a UNESCO World Heritage Site, it offers a glimpse into the social and industrial history of the region.

Brontë Parsonage Museum: Right in the heart of Haworth lies the former home of the Brontë family. If those walls could talk, they'd spill tales of Jane Eyre and Wuthering Heights being penned down. Meandering around, it's hard not to feel the literary vibes wafting in the air.

Royal Armouries Museum, Leeds: This isn't just another museum; it's a journey through time. From the knights of old to the samurai of Japan, it's a showcase of weapons and armor from different eras and parts of the world. And the best part? Live jousting and sword-fighting demonstrations.

Eureka! The National Children's Museum, Halifax: If you've got young adventurers in tow, this is the place to be. This interactive museum lets kids explore everything from the human body to the wonders of the digital world. It's all about hands-on learning and, trust me, it's not just for the little ones.

Hebden Bridge: A quirky, artistic town nestled amidst the Pennines. With its independent shops, vibrant arts scene, and the enchanting Hardcastle Crags nearby, it's a picturesque escape from the hustle and bustle.

The Piece Hall, Halifax: An architectural marvel, this Grade I listed building was once the center of the global wool trade. Today, it's a cultural and commercial hub, with boutique shops, lively events, and a testament to West Yorkshire's rich heritage.

Kirkstall Abbey: These Cistercian ruins on the banks of the River Aire are a serene relic of days gone by. With its sprawling parklands and the echoing arches of the abbey, it's easy to imagine robed monks wandering about, and legends of old coming alive in the hush of twilight.

North Yorkshire

York Minster: In the heart of the historic city of York, this gothic cathedral is an absolute showstopper. With its medieval stained-glass, stone masterpieces, and dizzying towers, it's no wonder it's one of the most magnificent cathedrals in Europe. Don't forget to climb up for a panoramic view of the city.

Whitby Abbey: Perched high on a cliff, the ruins of this 7th-century abbey are simply iconic. Also, very dark and brooding, but in a fantastic way. With its gothic spires, it's not only a sight to behold but also the inspiration for Bram Stoker's Dracula. Yes, Whitby is

where the famous Count first came ashore in England. A bit spooky, right?

Helmsley Walled Garden: Off the beaten path, these five-acre gardens are a delightful escape. Designed around fast-flowing streams, you'll find themed garden rooms, quirky sculptures, and even a "stumpery." Plus, with the Helmsley Castle ruins peeking over, it feels like a real-life secret garden.

The House of Trembling Madness, York: Alright, the name alone should pique your interest. This is actually one of the oldest buildings in York, now housing a quirky pub and shop. With medieval wooden beams, taxidermy, and an eclectic assortment of global beers, it's a hidden gem for those looking for something a little... different.

Robin Hood's Bay: A charming fishing village that feels like a step back in time. Its narrow, winding streets, picturesque cottages, and stunning coastline make it a delightful spot. And of course, with a name like that, legends abound—smugglers in particular. There's even a B&B called Smuggler's Cove nearby.

Mother Shipton's Cave: Located in Knaresborough, this is England's oldest visitor attraction, having been open since 1630. The cave is the legendary birthplace of Mother Shipton, a prophetess who is said to have predicted the future. The adjacent Petrifying Well is a unique natural phenomenon where objects turn to stone.

Rievaulx Abbey: Nestled in the Rye Valley, these are the impressive ruins of one of England's most powerful Cistercian monasteries. It's a peaceful location surrounded by woodland, and the remains tell a story of spiritual development, innovation, and eventual decline.

The Forbidden Corner: Located in the Yorkshire Dales, this is a unique labyrinth of tunnels, chambers, and surprises. It was originally built as a private folly but is now open to the public. It's a mesmerizing mix of statues, water features, and mysterious hideaways, making it a delightful adventure for both kids and adults.

The Holy Well of St. Helen in Stainland: This spot is set against the backdrop of the beautiful Yorkshire Dales. The well is said to have healing powers and has been a pilgrimage site for centuries. Surrounded by nature, it offers both spiritual solace and a touch of mysticism.

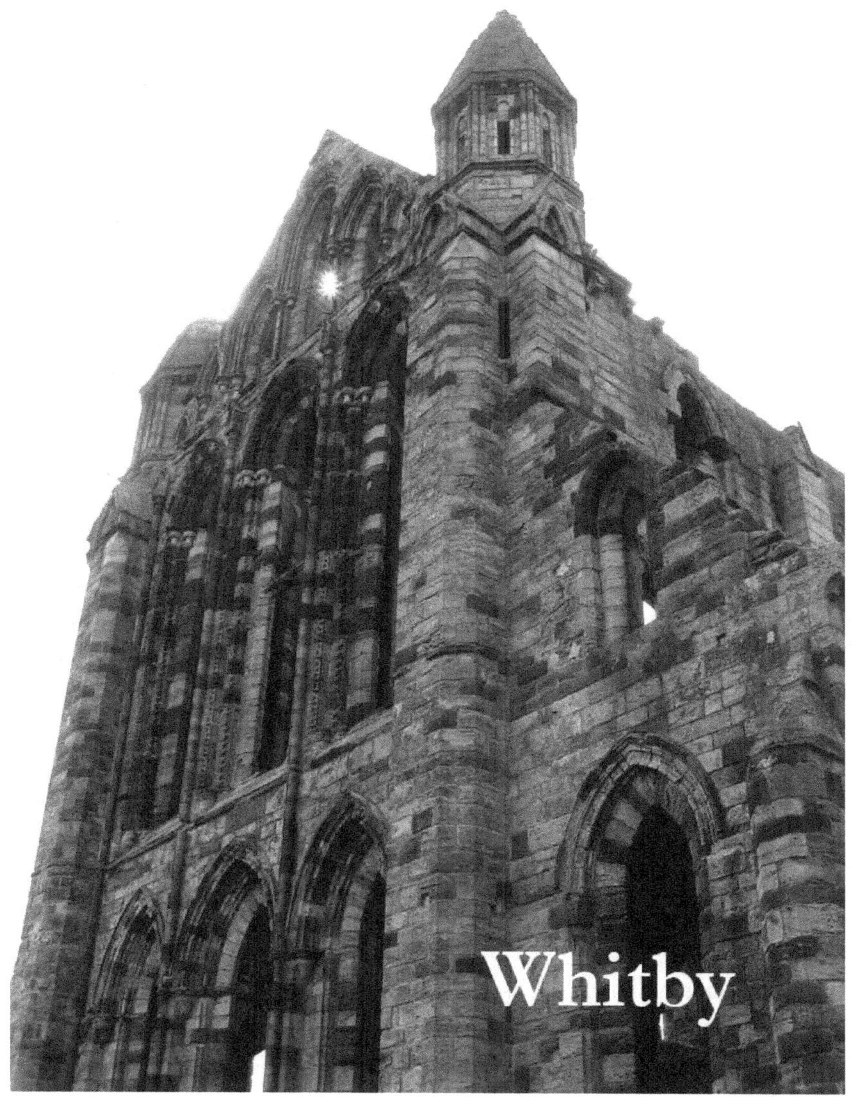

The Devil's Arrows: Located near Boroughbridge, these are three massive prehistoric monoliths that stand mysteriously in a row. Legend has it they were hurled by the devil from a nearby hill aiming for the town of Aldborough.

East Riding of Yorkshire

Flamborough Head: Offering dramatic chalk cliffs, this headland is one of the most prominent features on the northeast coast of England. The lighthouses and nearby Bempton Cliffs RSPB reserve, teeming with seabirds, make it a hotspot for nature lovers.

Beverley Minster: This Gothic masterpiece towers over the town of Beverley, a testament to medieval architecture. Its intricate stonework, majestic twin towers, and historic artifacts make it a must-visit. And did you know? It rivals many English cathedrals in size.

Spurn Point: A unique stretch of land reaching out into the Humber estuary. This slender spit with its tidal landscapes, shifting sands, and iconic lighthouse feels like a world removed from the mainland. Nature lovers, birdwatchers, or anyone seeking a moment of solitude, this is your sanctuary.

Burton Constable Hall: A splendid Elizabethan mansion surrounded by parkland. With its grand interiors and intriguing collections, it feels like stepping into a period drama. And who knows? You might just spot Mr. Darcy around the corner (or maybe just a very convincing re-enactor.).

Sewerby Hall and Gardens: Overlooking the dramatic cliffs of Bridlington Bay, this Georgian mansion is a treat. The hall is lovely, but the gardens? They're a patchwork of color, theme, and horticultural wonder. Plus, the little zoo on site might just make you feel you've landed in a whimsical world.

Bayle Museum, Bridlington: Housed in a former gateway to Bridlington Priory, this museum dives deep into local history, from its monastic origins to its time as a courtroom. And with its ancient stone walls, it's like a whisper from the past.

Rudston Monolith: Standing in the churchyard of All Saints' Church, this is the tallest standing stone in the UK. It dates back to the Late Neolithic period, and its purpose remains shrouded in mystery. Local legends speak of giants and ancient rituals. Standing in its shadow, you can't help but feel the weight of millennia.

EAST MIDLANDS

Derbyshire

Chatsworth House: This stately home, set amidst the Peak District, is the epitome of opulence. Whether you're marveling at its art collection, strolling through its sculpted gardens, or simply imagining yourself as Elizabeth Bennet in *Pride and Prejudice* (parts of which were filmed here), Chatsworth is an experience in regal delight.

The Heights of Abraham: A hilltop park reached by a delightful cable car ride, offering stunning views of the Derwent Valley. But the real magic? The caverns below. Ancient and mysterious, they offer a glimpse into the subterranean world and the history of the miners who once worked there.

Eyam—The Plague Village: This village is a poignant testament to resilience and sacrifice. When the plague hit in 1665, the villagers chose to quarantine themselves to prevent its spread. As you wander its streets, visit the museum and see the historic plaques, you'll be touched by the tales of heroism and humanity.

Cromford Mills: Nestled in the village of Cromford, this is the birthplace of the modern factory system. Part of the Derwent Valley Mills World Heritage site, it's a fascinating delve into the early days of the Industrial Revolution.

Nine Ladies Stone Circle: Located on Stanton Moor, this Bronze Age stone circle is surrounded by legend. As the name suggests, it's said that nine ladies were turned to stone for dancing on a Sunday. With ancient oaks and whispering winds, there's an undeniably magical aura about the place.

Pooles Cavern: This two-million-year-old limestone cave in Buxton is a subterranean wonderland of stalactites and stalagmites. Lit up to showcase its beauty, the caverns share tales of ancient Romans, Victorian adventurers, and curious explorers like yourself.

Peak District National Park: As the first national park in the UK, the Peak District offers a vast expanse of rolling hills, moorlands, and limestone dales. Perfect for hiking, cycling, or simply soaking in the panoramic views, it's a haven for outdoor enthusiasts.

Bolsover Castle: Overlooking the scenic countryside, this Stuart mansion is a lesser-known treasure with fairy-tale qualities. Its luxurious interiors, romantic terraces, and the impressive Venus Fountain are a few highlights.

Lumsdale Valley: Situated near Matlock, this wooded gorge houses a series of historic ruins, including watermills and old cottages. The cascading waterfalls and ancient stone buildings create a picturesque and atmospheric setting, offering a peaceful escape from the bustle of daily life.

Nottinghamshire

Nottingham Castle and Robin Hood Statue: Let's start with the obvious. Perched on Castle Rock, Nottingham Castle overlooks the city and offers a spectacular view. The castle has a tumultuous history, filled with sieges, battles, and royalty. And, of course, just a stone's throw away is the Robin Hood statue, celebrating Nottinghamshire's most legendary outlaw. Tip your hat to him and maybe, just maybe, you'll catch a glimmer of Maid Marian in the distance (not that she's in the original legends at all).

The City of Caves: Delve deep beneath the streets of Nottingham, and you'll discover a hidden world. These man-made caves date back to the Dark Ages and have served as homes, cellars, and even air-raid shelters. The sandstone caves are a unique underground experience, echoing tales of days gone by.

Sherwood Forest and the Major Oak: Ah, the legendary forest where Robin Hood and his merry men hid from the Sheriff. The Major Oak is said to be around 800-1,000 years old and, legend has it, served as the main hideout for our elusive hero. It's a mystical spot where ancient trees whisper tales of yore.

Wollaton Hall and Deer Park: Now, here's one of those hidden gems. This Elizabethan mansion is set in 500 acres of splendid parkland, complete with herds of red and fallow deer. Some might recognize the Hall as the Wayne Manor from the Batman film, "The Dark Knight Rises." A mix of natural beauty and Hollywood glamor, if you will.

The Museum of Nottingham Life at Brewhouse Yard: This lesser-known gem gives a fascinating insight into the lives of Nottingham's residents over the last 300 years. Nestled at the base of Castle Rock, this collection of 17th-century cottages paints a vivid picture of everyday life from Victorian times to the present day.

The Hemlock Stone: Now, for our dose of the mystical. This peculiar sandstone pillar stands at around 6 meters high, with legends and myths surrounding its origin. Some say it was thrown by the devil, aiming for a nearby abbey; others claim it's a sacred Druidic monument. Either way, there's an air of magic and mystery about this place that's sure to enchant.

Lincolnshire

Lincoln Cathedral: An iconic masterpiece, this cathedral soars over the city of Lincoln. For centuries, its towers held the title of the world's tallest building. With its intricate Gothic architecture and the mesmerizing labyrinth inlaid in its floor, it's a place where history and spirituality intertwine.

Belton House: A stately home that feels like it's sprung straight out of a Jane Austen novel. The mansion boasts opulent rooms, while the grounds are a verdant paradise replete with deer parks and serene lakes. Fancy a regal stroll?

St. Botolph's Church, Boston (The Boston Stump): This parish church isn't just any regular place of worship. Its tower, affectionately known as the "Boston Stump," offers panoramic views of the fens and even the North Sea on a clear day. Talk about heavenly views.

Gibraltar Point National Nature Reserve: With its dynamic landscapes of sand dunes, salt marshes, and lagoons, it's a sanctuary for a plethora of wildlife, especially birds. Nature lovers, prepare to have your hearts flutter.

Tattershall Castle: This medieval brick fortress feels like it's been plucked straight out of a fairy tale. With its spiraling staircases, gothic fireplaces, and legends of past inhabitants, there's an air of enchantment that's palpable. And if you climb to the battlements, the sweeping vistas of the Lincolnshire countryside will surely cast a spell on you.

The Kinema in the Woods: Located in Woodhall Spa, this unique cinema has been in operation since 1922. The Kinema offers a nostalgic cinema experience, with its classic interior, and even an interval during films where patrons can enjoy a traditional ice cream.

Natureland Seal Sanctuary in Skegness: More than just an attraction, this sanctuary rescues, rehabilitates, and releases injured seals from the Lincolnshire coast. Visitors can see the seals up close, as well as other marine creatures, tropical birds, and a collection of meerkats.

Leicestershire

Leicester Cathedral: This historic cathedral, right in Leicester's city centre, recently gained global attention as the final resting place of King Richard III. Rediscovered beneath a car park, his tale is one of historical sleuthing and medieval intrigue. As you explore the cathedral, you can't help but feel the weight of centuries gone by.

Bradgate Park: A sprawling park that tells tales of nature and history in tandem. Deer roam freely, rivers glisten, and in its midst stand the ruins of Bradgate House, the birthplace of Lady Jane Grey—England's nine-day queen. The combination of wildlife and history is simply enchanting.

The Great Central Railway: All aboard for a nostalgic journey on the UK's only double track, mainline heritage railway. From Loughborough to Leicester North, travel back in time as you chug through the picturesque countryside.

Mount St. Bernard Abbey: Tucked away near Coalville, here's one of the few Trappist monasteries in the UK. The monks not only offer a peaceful retreat but also brew the delicious Tynt Meadow Trappist beer – England's first Trappist ale.

Bosworth Battlefield Heritage Centre: Walk the grounds where King Richard III met his tragic end at the Battle of Bosworth in 1485. With re-enactments, guided walks, and a chance to relive a defining moment in English history, it's an experience that'll transport you back to the War of the Roses.

Rutland

Rutland Water: The jewel in Rutland's crown. This man-made reservoir isn't just a pretty face—it's a hub of activity. Whether you're sailing, birdwatching at its nature reserve, or simply ambling around its shores, the beauty of Rutland Water is undeniable.

Oakham Castle: This Norman hall may not resemble your traditional castle, but it has a quirky charm. What's especially intriguing is its unique collection of over 200 horseshoes, a tradition dating back centuries when visiting peers of the realm would gift a horseshoe to the Lord of the Manor.

Lyddington Bede House: This medieval bishop's palace was later transformed into an almshouse. It's a fascinating glimpse into both Tudor and Victorian times, with its historical chambers and manicured gardens offering a peaceful retreat.

Uppingham: One of Rutland's quaint market towns, Uppingham is a delightful maze of narrow streets, historic buildings, and antique shops. It's also home to Uppingham School, one of Britain's leading boarding schools with alumni that read like a who's who of British history.

Barnsdale Gardens: Created by the late Geoff Hamilton for BBC's "Gardeners' World," this is a garden lover's dream. With 38 individual gardens in one, it's a tapestry of horticultural designs and inspirations.

Wing Maze: A labyrinth turf-cut maze near the picturesque village of Wing. It's about 14 meters across, and is a type of maze typically associated with Theseus and the Minotaur.

Northamptonshire
Althorp House: Starting with a touch of aristocracy, this stately home has been the seat of the Spencer family for over 500 years. Besides its regal interiors and sprawling estate, it's also famously the childhood home and final resting place of Diana, Princess of Wales.

Silverstone Circuit: The pulse of adrenaline, the roar of engines – welcome to the home of the British Grand Prix. Whether you're an F1 enthusiast or just keen on feeling the rush, Silverstone promises high-octane excitement.

78 Derngate: This house in Northampton was reimagined in 1916 by the famed Scottish architect Charles Rennie Mackintosh. With its avant-garde design and Art Nouveau touches, it's a slice of architectural wonder right in the heart of town.

Canons Ashby: This Elizabethan manor house offers a tranquil escape with its historic interiors, serene gardens, and ancient priory church. It's like stepping into a postcard from the past.

The Eleanor Cross, Geddington: One of the twelve original crosses King Edward I had built in memory of his wife Eleanor. While these crosses once dotted the route her body took to its final resting place in London, the Geddington cross is one of the best preserved. A touching monument of love and history combined.

Kirby Hall: Let the walls of this Elizabethan country house share their tales. While partially roofless now, its beauty remains undeniable. The intricate gardens and the whispers of its ruins lend it an almost ethereal charm.

WEST MIDLANDS

Herefordshire

Hereford Cathedral: At the heart of Hereford lies this majestic cathedral, home to the legendary Mappa Mundi—a medieval map of the world. As you wander its historic halls, don't forget to visit the chained library, where ancient tomes have been safeguarded for centuries.

Berrington Hall: This Georgian mansion is an architectural gem with interiors that'll transport you straight to the elegance of the 18th century. The gardens, designed by Capability Brown, offer panoramic views of the Welsh mountains. A picturesque delight.

The Cider Route: When in Herefordshire, one should taste its famed cider. (my favorite) Wander through traditional orchards, visit cider mills, and sip on the golden nectar that this county is so celebrated for.

The Weir Garden: Nestled along the River Wye, this riverside garden is a haven of natural beauty. From vibrant bulbs in spring to the russet tones of autumn, every season offers a new reason to fall in love with this spot.

Arthur's Stone: This Neolithic burial chamber is steeped in legend. Rumored to be the very spot where King Arthur slew a giant, it's a place where history, myth, and the magic of the landscape intertwine. Feel the ancient energy, and who knows, maybe you'll hear whispers of old legends in the wind.

Brockhampton Estate: This medieval manorial complex may have once included a small village. The 14th-century timber framed house and Gatehouse have been restored to historical glory. Some marks on the gatehouse might be for keeping away evil spirits, and a "grey lady" is reported at times, in Victorian clothing.

The Black and White Village Trail: Dive deep into Herefordshire's heart with this trail that takes you through timber-framed villages straight out of a storybook. From Weobley to Eardisley, each village, with its black and white façade, is a picturesque pause in time.

Queenswood Country Park and Arboretum: An oasis of woodland and meadows, it boasts a collection of over 1,200 tree species from all over the globe. The panoramic views from various viewpoints are simply breathtaking, especially during autumn's fiery display.

Shropshire
Ironbridge Gorge: Dubbed the "Birthplace of the Industrial Revolution", this World Heritage site is home to ten museums. The iconic Iron Bridge itself, the first iron bridge of its kind in the world, stands as a testament to engineering and innovation.

Stokesay Castle: More a manor than a castle, this is one of the best-preserved medieval fortified manor houses in England. The timber-framed gatehouse and the stunning views from the tower make it feel like a setting straight out of a historical romance.

The Shropshire Hills: An Area of Outstanding Natural Beauty, these hills invite you for endless rambles. Whether you're scaling the Long Mynd or wandering through Carding Mill Valley, the panoramas are a treat for the soul.

Ludlow: This historic market town, with its Norman castle and timber-framed houses, is a gourmet's delight. From local farmers' markets to its famed food festival, Ludlow is a feast in every sense.

The Follies at Hawkstone Park: Dive into a magical world of grottoes, tunnels, and towering cliffs. This 18th-century fantasy woodland is our mystical pick. Legend speaks of hidden treasures and secret passageways. There's even the ghostly "White Lady" said to roam the grounds. With its mix of natural beauty and whispered tales, it's an adventure waiting to happen.

Blists Hill Victorian Town: Step back in time in this living museum. From the clinking of the blacksmith's forge to the aroma of freshly baked bread, experience life during the Victorian era. And yes, they have their own Victorian currency which you can use to shop.

Attingham Park: This elegant mansion, surrounded by its deer park, is a portal to the opulence of the 18th century. The walled garden, in particular, is a patchwork of colors and fragrances through the seasons.

Shrewsbury Abbey: Nestled in the heart of historic Shrewsbury, this Norman abbey is an absolute treat. Founded way back in 1083, it's seen centuries roll by, and while most of the original structure has sadly vanished, the remaining church is still a stunner. And as I am a huge fan of the books and the BBC series, I adored exploring the abbey, as it's famously featured in Ellis Peters' "Brother Cadfael" series.

Staffordshire
Alton Towers: Alton Towers isn't just one of the UK's top theme parks; it's a sprawling estate with gardens, mazes, and of course, those adrenaline-pumping rides. From the dizzying Smiler to the haunting Hex, there's a mix of fun and fright for everyone.

Lichfield Cathedral: This three-spired wonder is a true architectural gem. Delve into its medieval history, marvel at its stained-glass, and if you're feeling sprightly, why not climb for a view from the spires? The vista of Lichfield is well worth the ascent.

The Potteries: Stoke-on-Trent, Staffordshire's ceramic heartland, offers a chance to step into the world of pottery. From the iconic Wedgwood to the quirky Gladstone Pottery Museum, get your hands dirty and craft your masterpiece.

Shugborough Estate: This historic estate, once the home of the Earls of Lichfield, offers a delightful blend of mansion opulence, tranquil gardens, and a working farm. And if you're into photography, the late Patrick Lichfield's private apartments and collection are a treat.

Tamworth Castle: This Norman motte-and-bailey castle has seen a millennium of history. As you explore its rooms, each set in a different era, you'll journey from Saxon times right through to the Victorian age. Quite the time-travel experience.

The Roaches: These craggy gritstone edges and rock formations stand tall amidst the Peak District landscapes of Staffordshire. Legend says they are home to mermaids and magic, and the eerie, stunning Lud's Church chasm nearby only adds to the enchantment.

The Churnet Valley Railway: This is a stunning journey through Staffordshire's scenic spots. Aboard a heritage steam train, it's a delightful chug through the past, with the countryside unfurling like a vintage postcard.

Warwickshire

Warwick Castle: With its towering battlements and dramatic history, Warwick is every bit the quintessential castle. Don't forget to wander the peacock-filled gardens and, if you're feeling brave, delve into its spooky dungeons.

Stratford-upon-Avon: Stroll through timber-framed buildings, visit Shakespeare's birthplace, and if the stars align (or you book in advance), catch a play at the Royal Shakespeare Theatre. All the world's a stage here. The church where he is buried is a bit down the road from the main part of town. Visitors can read his epitaph, the last poem he wrote.

Kenilworth Castle: This castle has seen sieges, royal romances (Queen Elizabeth I was wooed here), and centuries of history. The Elizabethan Garden, recreated from the original designs, is a fragrant step back in time.

Compton Verney: This art gallery and park, housed in a Grade I listed mansion, boasts a captivating art collection amidst 120 acres of parkland. It's art, nature, and history all rolled into one.

The Rollright Stones: This ancient site is a complex of three Neolithic and Bronze Age megalithic monuments. Legends swirl around these stones – from tales of witches to kings turned to stone. Feel the magic in the air and maybe, just maybe, you'll uncover their secrets.

Hatton Locks: Dubbed the "Stairway to Heaven", this flight of 21 locks on the Grand Union Canal is a peaceful spot for canal boat watching, leisurely strolls, and soaking in the English countryside.

Anne Hathaway's Cottage: A lovely site in the quiet village of Shottery. This thatched-roofed, timber-framed cottage is where Shakespeare's wife spent her childhood. Wander the gardens, explore rooms filled with family artifacts, and bask in the romance of a bygone era.

West Midlands

Birmingham's Bullring & Grand Central: Dive straight into the modern hustle and bustle with one of the UK's largest shopping centres. With over 200 stores and the iconic, futuristic Selfridges Building, it's retail therapy with a twist.

Calanais II

Cadbury World: Unleash your inner child (or chocoholic). Located in the historic Bournville village, Cadbury World takes you on a delectable journey of chocolate-making, complete with tempting treats along the way.

Black Country Living Museum: Take a leap back in time in this open-air museum. Experience life during the Industrial Revolution with costumed characters, historic buildings, and even a trip down a mine. It's a vivid tableau of the past.

The Coffin Works: Located in Birmingham's Jewellery Quarter, this former coffin-fitting factory (yes, you read that right) offers a unique glimpse into the funerary trade and history. It's a touch macabre but utterly fascinating.

Sarehole Mill: This historic watermill, with ties to J. R. R. Tolkien, is said to have inspired the Shire in "The Lord of the Rings." Wander the grounds, and perhaps you'll find a hint of Middle-earth magic.

Warwickshire's Electric Railway: Okay, it's a tad outside the West Midlands County, but close enough to make the list. This charming heritage line, operated entirely by volunteers, offers a nostalgic journey through the English countryside.

Aston Hall: This Jacobean mansion, set amidst tranquil gardens, isn't just a historic gem. Rumor has it that it's haunted. With tales of Sir Thomas Holte and the Grey Lady, a visit might just send shivers down your spine.

Worcestershire

Worcester Cathedral: Towering over the River Severn, this majestic cathedral, with its Norman origins and Victorian restorations, is steeped in history. And the view from the tower? Simply breathtaking.

The Malvern Hills: Nature's very own playground. With a ridge that seems to stretch forever and panoramic views of the English countryside, it's perfect for those in search of fresh air and a bit of leg stretching. Did you know the hills also inspired the likes of Elgar and Tolkien?

The Commandery: Dive deep into Worcester's role in the English Civil War at this historic museum. With interactive exhibits and a garden that's a quiet oasis, it's a journey through the pages of history.

The Firs—Elgar's Birthplace: Nestled in the village of Lower Broadheath, discover the humble beginnings of Sir Edward Elgar, one of England's greatest composers. Let the notes of his compositions whisk you away as you explore his childhood home.

Broadway Tower: The Cotswolds might claim it, but since it's right on the border, we're sneaking it into our list. This "Saxon tower" offers panoramic views of up to 16 counties on a clear day. Plus, its park is home to a nuclear bunker and a herd of red deer.

Evesham Vale Light Railway: Hop aboard this delightful miniature steam train as it weaves through the scenic Evesham

Country Park. Particularly magical during their themed rides, like the Santa Specials.

Bambury Stone at Bredon Hill: Shaped like an elephant, these are the Midlands' answer to Stonehenge, albeit more quirky and completely free to explore. Bredon's ancient mystical rocks have stood the test of time, still standing tall in the wilds of Worcestershire.

SOUTHEAST

Berkshire

Windsor Castle: This historic castle was not only the Queen's favorite weekend home but also the world's oldest and largest inhabited castle. From the opulent State Apartments to the ancient Round Tower, it's every bit as majestic as you'd imagine.

The Savill Garden: Nestled within Windsor Great Park, this garden is a sensory delight across seasons – from spring's fresh blooms to autumn's fiery hues.

Reading Museum: Located in the heart of Reading, this museum boasts a slice of the Bayeux Tapestry, detailing the events leading up to the Norman conquest of England. There's also a Victorian schoolroom and a biscuit tin gallery—a nod to Reading's history as a biscuit-making town.

Bisham Abbey: Though now a National Sports Centre, parts of this stunning manor date back to the 12th century. With tales of the ghostly Lady Hoby, who's said to haunt its halls, it's a blend of beauty and eeriness.

Donnington Castle: Overlooking the town of Newbury, this 14th-century castle, though mostly in ruins, offers panoramic vistas of the surrounding countryside. Its gatehouse stands as a silent sentinel to history.

Frogmore House and Garden: A serene hideaway near Windsor Castle. Though lesser-known, its interiors are exquisite, and the garden, with its lily-laden lake, is nothing short of enchanting.

Buckinghamshire

Waddesdon Manor: Dive right into the opulence of the Rothschild family. This French château-style manor, surrounded by impeccable gardens, boasts a wine cellar, exquisite art collections, and hosts events year-round. The festive season, with the house decked out in Christmas grandeur, is particularly enchanting.

Bletchley Park: Decode the secrets of World War II. Once the top-secret home of the Codebreakers, it's where the genius minds, including Alan Turing, deciphered enemy codes. Visitors can explore the huts and learn about the birth of modern computing.

The Roald Dahl Museum and Story Centre: Step into the whimsical world of one of the greatest storytellers. Located in Great Missenden, where Dahl lived and wrote for over 36 years, it's an inspiring jaunt into the realms of Matilda, Charlie, and the BFG.

Hellfire Caves: Carved deep into the chalky hills of West Wycombe, these atmospheric caves have tales of the Hellfire Club, a group of 18th-century aristocrats with a penchant for the scandalous. Today, they beckon with their eerie allure and tales of old.

Hughenden Manor: This Victorian mansion, once home to Prime Minister Benjamin Disraeli, hides secrets of its time as a WWII map-making base. The gardens? A patchwork of color and fragrance.

Chenies Manor House: This Tudor gem, with its maze-like gardens and architectural delights, is steeped in history. From Royal visits to tales of espionage during the reign of Elizabeth I, there's much to uncover.

Burnham Beeches: This area was used in filming the Forbidden Forest for the Harry Potter movies, and contains the Druid's Oak, a 700-year old tree.

East Sussex

Beachy Head and the Seven Sisters: These chalky white cliffs, dramatically dropping into the sea, offer some of the most breathtaking coastal views in England. Their sheer scale and beauty are something to behold.

Battle Abbey: Can you hear the clanging of swords? This is the very site of the 1066 Battle of Hastings. Wander the ruins and dive deep into the day when history's course shifted on this very soil.

Bodiam Castle: This 14th-century moated castle, with its towers and battlements, is the stuff of knights and dragons. Just don't forget to draw the imaginary drawbridge behind you as you step in.

Charleston Farmhouse: Once the home of the Bloomsbury Group, which included Virginia Woolf and E.M. Forster, it's now a vibrant arts venue. The interiors, decorated by the artists themselves, radiate bohemian charm.

The Mermaid Inn, Rye: This atmospheric inn, with parts dating back to the 12th century, has a rich tapestry of history, including smuggling tales. Stay a night, if you dare, and let its creaky tales envelop you.

The Long Man of Wilmington: Carved into the South Downs, this mysterious chalk figure has been puzzling folks for centuries. Nobody's quite sure of its origins – ancient deity, symbol of fertility, or perhaps a playful work of more recent mischief? As you stand before it, ponder its tales and feel the aura of the unknown.

Drusillas Park: While primarily known as a family-friendly zoo, this place boasts beautiful gardens and play areas that make it a delightful stop for those traveling with little ones or just the young at heart.

Kent

Canterbury Cathedral: This UNESCO World Heritage Site, the heart of English Christianity, is an architectural marvel. Stained-glass windows, ancient stones, and the hauntingly beautiful crypt all sing tales from centuries past.

White Cliffs of Dover: Iconic and instantly recognizable, these chalky wonders stand sentinel, guarding the English coastline. Stroll along the cliffs, let the sea breeze tousle your hair, and soak in views that stretch clear across to France on a good day.

Leeds Castle: Dubbed "the loveliest castle in the world," this enchanting fortress, surrounded by a shimmering moat, is every bit a fairy-tale dream. With vast grounds, a maze, and even a falconry display, there's magic in the air. Note: this castle is not in the city of Leeds. We made that mistake in planning once.

Richborough Roman Fort: This ancient site marks the Romans' primary landing spot during their invasion of Britain in 43 CE. Amidst the ruins, feel the weight of millennia gone by.

Dungeness: This stark, shingle landscape, dotted with fishing huts, old rail tracks, and a looming nuclear power station, offers an eerie serenity. A true photographer's paradise, it's our second precious gem hidden away.

The Shell Grotto in Margate: Discovered in the 1830s, this subterranean passage is adorned with 4.6 million shells, creating intricate mosaics of unknown origin. The purpose and creators of this magical chamber remain a mystery, inviting speculations galore.

Bedgebury National Pinetum and Forest: An oasis for tree lovers and those seeking woodland solace. Home to the world's most comprehensive collection of conifers, it's a tapestry of greens, rusts, and golds, especially as autumn whispers through the boughs.

Oxfordshire

Oxford University and the Bodleian Library: The dreaming spires of Oxford are a world unto themselves. Wander through centuries-old colleges, take a peek at the Radcliffe Camera, and step into the hallowed halls of the Bodleian. Oh, and if enjoyed the Harry Potter movies, you'll spot a few film locations.

Blenheim Palace: Birthplace of Sir Winston Churchill and a UNESCO World Heritage Site, its grandeur, from the intricate tapestries to the vast grounds designed by Capability Brown, is sheer opulence personified.

Cotswold Wildlife Park and Gardens: A delightful mingling of landscaped gardens and a wide array of animals. From rhinos grazing against the backdrop of a historic manor to serene, wooded walks, this is nature's theater at its best.

The Rollright Stones: This ancient site, comprising a stone circle, burial chamber, and solitary standing stone, is steeped in legends. From tales of witches to kings turned to stone, there's an otherworldly aura that's palpable.

Harwell's Farmer Gow's: For those yearning for a touch of rural charm. This farm offers hands-on experiences, from feeding lambs to collecting chicken eggs. It's a patch of wholesome countryside joy.

Wallingford Castle Meadows: Once home to a royal castle, now only a few ruins remain. But these meadows by the River Thames offer scenic beauty, historic echoes, and are a perfect picnic spot.

Wantage: Often overshadowed by its famous neighbors, this market town is the birthplace of King Alfred the Great. Stroll its historic market square, visit the Vale & Downland Museum, and soak in the charm of a quintessential English town.

Surrey

Guildford Castle: While today it's mostly ruins, the gardens are lush and the tower view over Guildford is a treat. Can you hear the echoes of history as you meander through?

The Surrey Hills: An Area of Outstanding Natural Beauty, these hills are just calling out for a long walk. Box Hill, made famous by Jane Austen's "Emma," offers panoramic views that might just steal your breath away.

Brooklands Museum: Dive into the world of motorsport and aviation. As the birthplace of British motorsport and aviation, Brooklands is teeming with exciting exhibits, from vintage cars to a Concorde.

Watts Chapel: Nestled in the village of Compton, this Arts and Crafts-style chapel is adorned with intricate designs, all envisioned by Mary Watts, wife of the Victorian artist G.F. Watts. Every inch tells a tale.

RHS Garden Wisley: A slice of horticultural heaven. As the flagship garden of the Royal Horticultural Society, Wisley is a mesmerizing blend of formal gardens, woodland paths, and exotic plant displays. It is pure poetry for plant lovers.

The Silent Pool: This spring-fed lake is surrounded by legends. The most enduring tale is of a woodcutter's daughter, chased by King John, who drowned in its still waters. Some say on quiet nights, her ghostly figure can be glimpsed.

The Sculpture Park: This is an outdoor gallery like no other — a 10-acre site filled with over 600 sculptures, nestled amidst ponds, heathland, and woodland. It's art and nature dancing together in perfect harmony.

West Sussex

Arundel Castle: As quintessentially English as it gets. Towering over the River Arun, this medieval castle is a timeline of architecture, from Norman keeps to Victorian bedrooms. And don't miss the marvelous gardens.

The Wittering and Bracklesham Bay: These sandy shores are a seaside haven. Whether you're building sandcastles, windsurfing, or just soaking up the sun, this is coastal rejuvenation at its best.

Petworth House and Park: This stately home boasts an impressive collection of artworks, including pieces by Turner. The parkland, designed by Capability Brown, is an open invitation to wander and wonder.

Cowdray Ruins: Nestled in Midhurst, these atmospheric ruins tell tales of Tudor banquets, royal visits, and a mysterious fire. A place where history's whispers come alive.

Weald and Downland Living Museum: With over 50 historic buildings, from windmills to timber-framed houses, it's a fascinating journey from the Anglo-Saxon era to Victorian times.

Bignor Roman Villa: Here's a secret from antiquity. Unearthed at the foot of the South Downs, this Roman villa is home to some of the most well-preserved mosaics in England. It's a mosaic of history and art, quite literally.

Chanctonbury Ring: This ancient hill fort, crowned with a ring of trees, is steeped in legends. From Roman temples to tales of the Devil himself, there's an air of enchantment (and maybe a touch of eerie) that clings to this hilltop.

Hampshire
Winchester Cathedral: This stunning gothic cathedral, one of the largest in Europe, holds within its hallowed walls tales of kings, saints, and even a diver who saved its foundations. Plus, Jane Austen fans can pay their respects at her final resting place here.

The New Forest: A mosaic of heathlands, ancient woodlands, and quaint villages. Whether you're spotting wild ponies, exploring the trails, or simply picnicking amidst nature, it's a rejuvenating retreat. If you want a real treat, read Edward Rutherfurd's novel, The Forest, before exploring.

Mary Rose Museum, Portsmouth: This museum showcases Henry VIII's flagship, the Mary Rose, which sank in 1545 and was raised from the seabed in 1982. It's like peering through a time capsule.

Gilbert White's House & The Oates Collection: Home of the pioneering naturalist, Gilbert White, it's a delightful dive into 18th-century natural history. The Oates Collection celebrates explorers Frank and Lawrence Oates, making it a treasure trove for history and nature enthusiasts.

Hinton Ampner: An elegant country house set amidst splendid gardens, it's also our second hidden gem. While the house boasts tales of ghostly occurrences, the gardens shimmer with beauty across seasons.

Highclere Castle: If you're a fan of Downton Abbey, this place is very familiar. While the house is closed to the public, you can get a good view of the castle via a path on Beacon Hill.

The Rufus Stone: Marking the spot where King William II, known as Rufus, was allegedly killed in a hunting accident in 1100, this stone is shrouded in mystery and legend. Was it truly an accident, or a well-plotted assassination? The forest keeps its secrets.

Buckler's Hard: Step back in time in this 18th-century shipbuilding village on the banks of the Beaulieu River. With its charming Georgian cottages and maritime museum, it's a picturesque peek into the past.

Isle of Wight
The Needles: These dramatic chalk stacks, rising from the sea, are an absolute spectacle. And the candy-colored lighthouse perched

at the end is picture-perfect. A chairlift ride offers mesmerizing views and a tinge of thrill.

Osborne House: This Italian-style palazzo gives a fascinating glimpse into the royal life, with lavish rooms and manicured gardens. Queen Victoria's private retreat offers a fantastic private beach, too.

Carisbrooke Castle: History and bunnies, anyone? Once a royal prison for King Charles I, this historic castle now has charming gardens and the famous well-house where donkeys demonstrate age-old water-fetching techniques. And yes, there's a colony of adorable bunnies here.

Shanklin Chine: This lush ravine, a haven of waterfalls, leafy canopies, and winding paths, is especially magical when illuminated in the evenings. Nature's serenade at its finest, and often touted as the island's oldest tourist attraction.

The Mottistone Gardens: Not only does it boast vibrant flora, but also the intriguing Mottistone Long Stone, hinting at ancient rituals and gatherings. History and horticulture, hand in hand.

Ventnor Botanic Garden: Nestled in the island's unique microclimate, it's a plant lover's paradise with species that can't be found anywhere else in the UK. The garden's subtropical and exotic collections will make you question if you're still in England.

Tennyson Down: Named after the poet Lord Tennyson, who often wandered here, this ridge offers panoramic views that are nothing short of poetic. Legend says the whispers of old poems and fae-folk tales float in the wind. Can you catch one?

SOUTHWEST

Dorset

Jurassic Coast: This UNESCO World Heritage Site is a geologist's dream and a wanderer's paradise. From the iconic Durdle Door arch to the layered cliffs of Lulworth Cove, it's a journey through 185 million years of Earth's history.

Corfe Castle: Rise above the mist with this evocative ruin. Once a royal stronghold, its battlements now bear witness to centuries of intrigue and rebellion. The views from atop are simply spellbinding.

The Cerne Abbas Giant: A curious chalk figure etched into the hillside and maintained by the locals, this giant with his... ahem, prominent feature, is steeped in mystery. Is he ancient? Is he more recent? He's certainly a talking point.

Tyneham Village: Dubbed the village that time forgot, it was evacuated during World War II and has remained uninhabited since. Walking its abandoned streets is like stepping into a poignant time capsule.

Athelhampton House and Gardens: Tucked away near Puddletown, this a quintessential English manor with history-soaked rooms and gardens that look plucked from the pages of a storybook. It's history and horticulture in harmony.

The Blue Pool: A magical spot near Wareham. Thanks to the clay beneath, the water here shimmers in changing shades of blue and turquoise. Surrounded by woods, this serene place is tranquility encapsulated.

Tolpuddle Martyrs Museum: Harking back to a crucial chapter in the history of workers' rights, this museum commemorates the six Tolpuddle men who dared to demand fair wages and changed the course of English social history.

Somerset

Glastonbury Abbey and Tor: Can't begin Somerset without Glastonbury, even without the muddy music festival. The abbey is steeped in Arthurian legends, said to be King Arthur's burial place, and might be the heart of Avalon. The mystical Tor with its iconic tower offers panoramic views and has been a site of pilgrimage and mystery for eons.

Bath: Time travel to Roman and Georgian times. The Roman Baths are a testament to ancient luxury, while the Georgian architecture, like the Royal Crescent, showcases 18th-century grandeur. If you go into the spa itself, you can take a sip of Bath's mineral-rich waters.

Cheddar Gorge: Stand in awe of England's largest gorge with its dramatic cliffs and subterranean stalactite show caves. And, of course, grab some of the world-famous Cheddar cheese right from its source.

Dunster Castle: Nestled on a wooded hill, this ancient castle turned lavish country home boasts beautiful gardens and views that stretch to the Bristol Channel. Its history is told through tapestries, timber and terraces.

The Shoe Museum, Street: Walk (pun intended) through over a thousand shoes, from Egyptian sandals to modern sneakers. A quirky testament to the county's footwear industry, primarily driven by the Clarks family.

Wells: Despite being England's smallest city, the majestic Wells Cathedral with its unique scissor arches and the ancient Bishop's Palace, complete with moat and drawbridge, are sheer visual delights.

Bristol

SS Great Britain: This magnificent ship, now a museum, once ruled the waves as the world's largest passenger steamship. Today, it paints tales of Victorian seafaring adventures.

Bristol Balloon Fiesta: Do you dream of skies speckled with vibrant hot air balloons? Every summer, the skies over Bristol come alive with colors, sheer poetry in motion.

Clifton Suspension Bridge: This iconic bridge, spanning the Avon Gorge, isn't just an engineering marvel, but also offers views that could inspire sonnets.

Banksy Street Art Tour: Delve into the world of the elusive street artist, Banksy. Wander Bristol's streets to discover some of his earliest and most iconic works. It's art, activism, and mystery rolled into one.

The Lido: A hidden oasis in the heart of the city. This restored Victorian swimming pool also houses a spa, restaurant, and poolside bar. Dive in, the water (and the vibes) are just fine.

The Red Lodge Museum: Wander through this Tudor/ Elizabethan house, replete with its oak-paneled rooms and hidden gardens. Time-travel, anyone?

The Cabot Tower: Nestled in the lovely Brandon Hill Park, this tower offers panoramic views of the city. But it's at dawn or twilight, with the city lights twinkling and the soft glow of the horizon, that the place truly feels enchanted.

Gloucestershire

Gloucester Cathedral: An architectural marvel, this cathedral has seen over 1,300 years of history. Its cloisters might tickle your memory – they've served as the hallowed hallways of Hogwarts in the Harry Potter films.

The Forest of Dean: This ancient woodland is a sylvan dream, where trails weave through trees, leading to secret glades and shimmering ponds. It's said that J. R. R. Tolkien took inspiration from these woods for Middle-earth's forests.

Cheltenham: Known for its horse racing and literary festivals, this Regency spa town, with its leafy promenades and Georgian architecture, are perfect for a leisurely stroll.

Berkeley Castle: A place where history is etched into every stone. This medieval fortress has been the seat of the Berkeley family for over 850 years. Rumor has it, it's where King Edward II met his gruesome end.

The Cotswold Way: This 102-mile-long footpath is a hidden ribbon of beauty that meanders through picturesque villages, rolling hills, and offers vistas that will make your heart sing.

Cotswold Lavender: Fields upon fields of purple lavender stretching as far as the eye can see. Visit in summer, and it's like stepping into a fragrant dream.

Wiltshire

Stonehenge: This is the elephant in the room of mystical sites in England. These iconic ancient stones, standing stoically on Salisbury

Plain, are steeped in millennia of mystery. There are many theories about why they were built; about as many as there are theorists.

Avebury Stone Circle: This is the world's largest prehistoric stone circle, and you're free to wander among its ancient stones. Touch the sarsens, feel the pulses of history, and perhaps, just perhaps, a hint of magic. Or even have a pint at the pub in the middle of the circle.

Salisbury Cathedral: Gothic splendor at its finest. Home to the best-preserved copy of the Magna Carta, this cathedral's spire touches the heavens, and its cloisters whisper tales of old.

The Kennet Long Barrow: Dive deeper into the ancient at this Neolithic tomb. Older than Stonehenge, it's a passage into the past, both literally and figuratively. Inside, the external world seems eerily absent.

Lacock Village: A village where time has paused. With its timber-framed cottages and medieval streets, it's no wonder location scouts (like Downton Abbey) have been spellbound.

Castle Combe: Often dubbed "the prettiest village in England," its honey-colored stone houses and tranquil ambience make it the perfect antidote to modern hustle.

Silbury Hill: The largest man-made mound in Europe, its purpose remains an enigma. Was it a spiritual site? A territorial marker? Or perhaps a place where the veils between worlds were thin?

Devon

Dartmoor National Park: Imagine a vast expanse of wild moorland, granite tors reaching for the sky, and free-roaming Dartmoor ponies. This landscape is hauntingly beautiful, steeped in folklore and natural splendor.

Exeter Cathedral: A masterpiece of Gothic architecture. Its vaulted ceiling is a marvel, and if those ancient stones could talk, the stories it would tell. Don't miss the astronomical clock, where centuries have ticked away.

The English Riviera: Comprising Torquay, Paignton, and Brixham, it's a slice of coastal charm. Sun-kissed beaches, Victorian piers, and seafood to die for. Remember, in Devon, it's cream first, then jam on those scones. And if you're a fan of Fawlty Towers, Torquay is where the show was set.

Clovelly: A privately owned village where time seems to stand still. Cobbled streets, no cars, just donkeys and sledges to transport goods. Descend its steep lanes and you're rewarded with a shimmering harbor.

Lundy Island: A true treasure off the Devon coast. A haven for wildlife, with puffins, seals, and a backdrop of rugged beauty. It's also steeped in smuggling legends and tales of pirates.

Buckland Abbey: This historic gem was once home to Sir Francis Drake, the famed navigator. Explore the manor, the gardens, and perhaps, if you're lucky, stumble upon the reputedly cursed Drake's Drum.

Wistman's Wood: Delve into this ancient oak woodland on Dartmoor. Twisted trees, moss-covered boulders, and an atmosphere of enchantment. Legends speak of Druids, ghosts, and supernatural beings lurking in its midst, including "Wisht Hounds" with red eyes and a taste for blood, and knots of super-venomous adders.

Cornwall

St. Michael's Mount: This tidal island, crowned by a medieval castle, is steeped in legend. Accessible by a causeway at low tide, it's as if you're walking a path between worlds.

The Eden Project: Step into the world's largest indoor rainforest. Nestled in giant biomes, discover plants from across the globe. It's a journey from the Amazon to the Mediterranean, all within Cornwall's embrace.

Tintagel Castle: Legendary birthplace of King Arthur, these ruins perched on Cornwall's dramatic north coast whisper tales of knights, sorcery, and Merlin's magic. However, it's actually a ruin of a Norman castle, all romanticism aside.

Porthcurno Beach: A gem with golden sands cradled between cliffs. But the true hidden marvel is the Minack Theatre, an open-air Amphitheatre etched into granite, with the ocean as its backdrop.

Lost Gardens of Heligan: Nature's secret wonderland. Once forgotten, these gardens were rediscovered and restored, revealing Victorian splendors, jungle walks, and sculptures that seem to breathe with life.

Boscastle: A charming harbor village that's also home to the Museum of Witchcraft and Magic. Dive into the mystical, exploring artifacts and tales of old-world magics.

Bodmin Moor: The heart of Cornish magic. Amidst its sweeping landscapes stands the Dozmary Pool, said to be the resting place of King Arthur's Excalibur, guarded by the Lady of the Lake.

EAST OF ENGLAND

Essex
Colchester Castle: Britain's oldest recorded town. This Norman castle, constructed on the foundations of a Roman temple, offers a time-touched exploration of history from the Romans to the Normans.

Southend-on-Sea: The longest pleasure pier in the world, amusement arcades, and the promise of fish & chips by the waves.

Beth Chatto Gardens: For a slice of natural serenity, wander these beautiful gardens. Created by the legendary plants-woman Beth Chatto, it's a testament to harmonizing plants with their environment.

Epping Forest: An ancient woodland on London's doorstep, it's a haven for nature lovers. With its history as a royal hunting ground, expect to find ancient pollards, diverse habitats, and maybe even a deer or two.

Layer Marney Tower: This Tudor palace, despite being unfinished, boasts of being the tallest Tudor gatehouse in England. Its ornate terracotta work and views over the Blackwater estuary are simply enchanting.

Mersea Island: Essex's coastal gem, renowned for its oysters. But beyond seafood, it's a realm of sandy beaches, colorful beach huts, and boat-filled creeks. A perfect escape from the world.

Hertfordshire

St Albans Cathedral: Immerse yourself in this majestic cathedral city. With its blend of Roman relics and stunning medieval architecture, the cathedral (or "abbey," as locals fondly call it) is a testament to faith, time, and artistry.

Hatfield House: Step into Jacobean grandeur. Once the childhood home of Queen Elizabeth I, this estate now offers exquisite gardens, historic mementos, and even the famous Rainbow Portrait of the queen herself.

Knebworth House: Knebworth has rocked to the beats of legends like Led Zeppelin and Pink Floyd. Gothic architecture, sprawling gardens, and that undeniable aura of rock-n-roll.

De Havilland Aircraft Museum: A gem for aviation enthusiasts. Dedicated to the legacy of Geoffrey de Havilland, it houses iconic aircraft like the Mosquito and the Comet, narrating stories of the skies.

Ashridge Estate: Spanning 5,000 acres, it's a haven of woodlands, chalk downlands, and deer-filled meadows. And in spring, it becomes a bluebell spectacle straight out of a dream.

Scott's Grotto: Located in Ware, this series of interconnected chambers is adorned with shells, flints, and colored glass. The grotto's purpose remains a mystery, making it all the more enchanting.

The Rex Cinema, Berkhamsted: Restored to its 1938 glory, it's often regarded as one of the most beautiful cinemas in the UK. Watch a film here, and it's not just a movie; it's a nostalgic embrace.

Bedfordshire

Woburn Abbey and Safari Park: Explore the dual experience of historic grandeur and wild encounters. The ancestral home of the Dukes of Bedford, this abbey offers art, antiques, and 3,000 acres of deer park. And just a stone's throw away is A safari park where majestic creatures roam.

Luton Hoo: An elegant country estate that feels like a step back into aristocratic luxury. With its sprawling gardens designed by Capability Brown and a mansion that's witnessed royalty, it's a dose of Downton Abbey-esque allure.

The Shuttleworth Collection: For the aviation aficionados, this unique aeronautical and automotive museum in Old Warden Park showcases vintage aircraft, classic cars, and a slice of Edwardian elegance.

Moggerhanger Park: A Georgian Grade I listed country house designed by the renowned architect Sir John Soane. Its serene parkland and historic rooms whisper tales of yesteryears.

Priory Country Park: An oasis in Bedford, this park offers lakes, woodlands, and meadows. Perfect for a leisurely stroll, birdwatching, or simply basking in nature's embrace.

The Panacea Museum: Dive into the world of the Panacea Society, a religious community awaiting the end of the world in Bedford during the early 20th century. A curious blend of garden beauty and unique history.

Houghton House: These evocative ruins, perched on a hill, offer views over the Bedfordshire countryside. With ties to the tale of John Bunyan's "Pilgrim's Progress," there's an aura of age-old tales and legends enveloping the place.

Cambridgeshire

University of Cambridge: This centuries-old institution isn't just a hub of academic brilliance, but a mosaic of history, art, and architecture. Wander its colleges, admire the Bridge of Sighs, and let the musings of great minds of yore envelop you.

Ely Cathedral: A stunning masterpiece rising from the fens. Known as the "Ship of the Fens," this grand cathedral boasts a unique octagonal tower and hosts regular musical concerts that echo with ethereal beauty.

The Fitzwilliam Museum: Dive into a treasure trove of art and antiquities. From Egyptian mummies to masterpieces by Titian and Picasso, it's like leafing through the vibrant pages of global history.

Wicken Fen Nature Reserve: One of Britain's oldest nature reserves, it's a wetland wonder. Wander boardwalk trails, spot dragonflies, and feel the pulse of Cambridgeshire's wild heart.

Anglesey Abbey: A Jacobean-style house with gardens that are a delight in every season. But the true magic is the working watermill and the winter garden, where silver birches and white narcissi paint a snowy spectacle.

The Orchard Tea Garden: An unassuming treasure in Grantchester. Picture this: sipping tea under apple trees, a tradition cherished by the likes of Virginia Woolf and Rupert Brooke.

Grafham Water: This serene reservoir offers waterside walks, but as the mists roll in, and the waters shimmer under twilight, there's an undeniable whisper of the mystical in the air.

Norfolk

Norwich Cathedral: An architectural gem in the heart of a bustling city. With its soaring spire, this Norman cathedral is a sanctuary of serenity, history, and the occasional peregrine falcon sighting. And home to Julian of Norwich, an anchoress from the 14th-15th century well-known as a mystic.

The Norfolk Broads: Nature's sprawling labyrinth. Miles of navigable waterways weave through windmills, quaint villages, and reed beds. Perfect for boating adventures or simply soaking in the tranquil vistas.

Holkham Hall & Beach: An 18th-century Palladian mansion meets an untouched stretch of golden sands. Whether it's art and history or dunes and pine woods, Holkham offers a symphony of experiences.

Blakeney Point: A dance of tides and seals. This nature reserve is a haven for birdwatchers and home to both gray and common seals. Ready for some seal-spotting amidst shifting sands?

Blickling Estate: This Jacobean mansion has stories etched into its walls – tales of Anne Boleyn's ghost, secret tunnels, and gardens that burst with color and history.

Binham Priory: Ruined yet resplendent, its atmosphere is thick with tales of yore. As the sun dips and shadows play, it's easy to imagine the harmonies of monks echoing through time.

The Shell Museum, Glandford: An unexpected treasure trove, this tiny place is brimming with shells from around the world, it's a quirky testament to one man's passion and the wonders of the natural world.

Suffolk

Sutton Hoo: Dive deep into the mysteries of the Anglo-Saxons, an actual treasure trove. This archeological site revealed an undisturbed ship burial, with treasures that gleam with tales of ancient kings and distant voyages.

Bury St Edmunds: A jewel of a town, where the magnificent cathedral and ruins of an abbey stand testament to faith and time. Stroll the Abbey Gardens and let history wrap around you.

Aldeburgh: With its pebble beach, fresh seafood, and the looming sculpture of the Scallop dedicated to Benjamin Britten, it's a blend of nature, art, and taste.

Lavenham: Often termed England's best-preserved medieval village, its crooked timbered houses, the magnificent church, and quaint lanes feel like a scene from a historical tapestry.

Orford Ness: An eerie, isolated spit of land. Once a top-secret military testing site, now a nature reserve, its juxtaposition of natural beauty and remnants of Cold War installations is hauntingly captivating.

The House in the Clouds: A tucked-away treasure in Thorpeness. This whimsical house, seemingly floating above the trees, promises views that stretch out to infinity and perhaps, a pinch of magic.

Rendlesham Forest: Known for the famous UFO incident in 1980, the forest hums with tales of otherworldly encounters. Whether you believe in extraterrestrial visitors or not, the forest's beauty is undeniable.

LONDON

Greater London

The Tower of London: We're going headfirst into history with tales of kings, queens, and the occasional beheading. This iconic fortress houses the Crown Jewels, whispers of Anne Boleyn's ghost, and ravens that hold the fate of England.

The British Museum: A passport to the world, all under one roof. Saunter past the Rosetta Stone, stand in the shadow of the Elgin Marbles, and journey through cultures and epochs.

Camden Market: From gothic garb to street food from around the world, this bustling marketplace is a kaleidoscope of tastes, sounds, and styles.

Daunt Books: Nestled in Marylebone, this Edwardian shop dedicated to travelers is a sanctuary for book lovers. Oak galleries, skylights, and curated collections make it more than just a bookstore.

Little Venice: A tucked-away treasure. Wander along its picturesque canals, hop onto a narrowboat, and find quaint waterside cafes. It's a slice of serenity amidst the urban rush.

The Seven Noses of Soho: Fancy a quirky quest? Scattered around Soho are seven sculpted noses created by artist Rick Buckley. Legend has it, finding all seven brings infinite wealth.

The Hunterian Museum: Explore this lesser-known gem filled with medical specimens, fascinating oddities, and even the skeleton of the "Irish Giant." It's a dance of wonder and eerie beauty.

City of London

St. Paul's Cathedral: Crowned by its iconic dome, Sir Christopher Wren's masterpiece offers not just spiritual solace but panoramic views of London from its Golden Gallery. Whispering sweet nothings in the Whispering Gallery is a must-try.

The Monument: A towering tribute to the Great Fire of London, 1666. Climb its winding 311 steps, and you're rewarded with sweeping views and a certificate to prove your feat.

Leadenhall Market: With its ornate roof and Victorian elegance, this covered market feels like stepping into a Dickensian dream. And if it seems familiar, it did feature as Diagon Alley in Harry Potter.

Postman's Park: Hidden amidst the urban hustle, this serene spot pays tribute to heroic self-sacrifice—commemorating individuals who died while saving others. A touching testament to everyday heroes.

The Temple of Mithras: Dive deep beneath modern London to discover this ancient Roman temple. Rediscovered in the 1950s, it offers a glimpse into the mysticism and daily life of Roman Londinium.

The Seven City Dragons: Dragons mark the boundaries of The City, standing guard against potential threats. Seek them out and perhaps, just perhaps, you'll find yourself ensnared in their age-old enchantments.

CONCLUSION

I do hope you enjoyed your journey through the hills, dales, and coastlines of England. The land is so enriched by history, legend, and myth, a stunning jewel on the crown of Europe.

There is a passion of place and of people in this land, one that is strong and deep, though sometimes austere and silent as well. It is manifest in the manner of the people, the strength of the hills, and the beauty in the art and architecture.

If you travel anywhere, it helps, I believe, to have some sense of history, some knowledge of the myths and beliefs of the land. I believe this increases the magic the land reflects into the true traveler.

Whether you are visiting to enjoy the beautiful gardens, the charming pubs, the hidden magic places, the stunning architecture, or the megalithic monuments of England, you will not be disappointed. It is a place to hold dear; a place to make memories to treasure and relish; a stunning place of magic and mystery.

When the magical secrets of The Emerald Isle beckon, will she survive answering the call?

Can Valentia embrace her elusive legacy while protecting those she loves?

Start reading *Legacy of Hunger* to trace a family treasure today.

THANK YOU

Thank you so much for enjoying this guide. If you've enjoyed the story, please consider leaving a review so other readers can discover England's hidden treasures.

If you would like to get updates, sneak previews, sales, and **FREE STUFF**, please sign up for my newsletter.

**See all the books available
through Green Dragon Publishing at
www.GreenDragonArtist.com/Books**

Read Now

RESOURCES

WEBSITE RESOURCES

General England Information

- Green Dragon Artist, http://www.greendragonartist.com, my own website dedicated to travel, books, and art.
- England, http://www.England.org— A great resource for all things English.

Mythical, Mystical, Historical or Hidden Places

- Celtic Myth Podshow, https://podcasts.apple.com/us/podcast/celtic-myth-podshow/id272848127 — dramatizations of Celtic myths.
- Powerful Places, http://www.powerfulplaces.com — a great set of books and a blog for spiritual places in the British Isles.
- Sacred Texts, http://www.sacred-texts.com – a guide to tales from William Yeats, Lady Gregory and many others.
- Stone Pages, http://www.stonepages.com — a guide to stone circles and standing stones.
- Thin Place, http://www.thinplace.net — a guide to spiritual places.
- UNESCO World Heritage Centre, http://whc.unesco.org — listing of World Heritage sites.

Travel Related Sites

- Auto Europe, https://www.autoeurope.com/ — Car Rental.
- Enterprise Car Rental, http://www.enterprise.com.
- Expedia, http://www.expedia.com .
- Fodor's Forums, http://www.fodors.com/community — great help (and some snarky advice) from others who have been there.
- Google Maps, https://maps.google.com.
- Green Traveller, http://www.greentraveller.co.uk — for those that prefer low carbon holidays.
- Insure My Trip, http://www.insuremytrip.com — to compare travel insurance plans.
- Listed properties of the UK, http://www.list.co.uk.
- BritRail, http://www.Britrail.co.uk.
- English pubs, http://www.insiders-England-guide.com/EnglishPubs.html.
- Seat Guru, http://www.seatguru.com — find out which seats are best.
- Slow Travel, https://www.smartertravel.com/art-slow-travel — for those who wish to travel at a slower pace.
- Traditional Music and Song, http://www.thesession.org.
- Trip Advisor, — for researching the B&Bs, hotels, and sites.
- Via Michelin, http://www.viamichelin.com — great for planning routes and times.
- Unusual places to stay, http://www.quirkyaccom.com.

Discount Sources
- Airfare Watchdog, — for discount airfare.
- English Heritage Pass, https://www.english-heritage.org.uk/visit/overseas-visitors/.
- Flyertalk, http://www.flyertalk.com — for those who travel frequently.
- Kayak, http://www.kayak.com.
- Last Minute Travel, — for last minute airfare deals.
- Lonely Planet, http://www.lonelyplanet.com — good all-round site, especially for tight budgets.

- National Heritage Membership, http://www.britainexpress.com/England/index.html.
- Student Universe, — for student and teacher travel.
- Travel Zoo, http://www.travelzoo.com — for discount airfare.
- Veteran's Advantage, http://www.veteransadvantage.com— for veteran travel.

Photography Sources

- DP Review, http://www.dpreview.com – to compare cameras.
- Lulu, http://www.lulu.com – for book and calendar printing.
- Simply Canvas, http://www.simplycanvas.com – for photographic printing.
- White House Custom Copies, – for photographic printing.

Print Resources

- Ashmore, P.J., Neolithic and Bronze Age England: An Authoritative and Lively Account of an Enigmatic Period of English Prehistory, Batsford, 2003.
- Campbell, John Gregorson, The Gaelic Otherworld, Birlinn, Ltd., 2012.
- Matthews, John. Celtic Myths and Legends, Pitkin Guides, 2001. McNeill, F. Marian, The Silver Bough, Canongate, 2001.
- Pryor, F., Britain B.C.: Life in Britain and Ireland before the Romans, Harper Collins, 2003.
- Sjoestedt, Marie-Louise. Gods and Heroes of the Celts. London, 1949. Translation by Miles Dillon of Sjoestedt's Dieux et hèros des Celtes. Paris, 1940.
- Stewart, R.J. Celtic Gods, Celtic Goddesses. Blandford Press, 1992.
- Stewart, R.J. Celtic Myths, Celtic Legends. Blandford Press, 1996.
- Sykes, Bryan, Saxons, Vikings and Celts: The Genetic Roots of Britain and Ireland, W.W. Norton & Company, 2007.

DEDICATION

I would like to dedicate this book to my parents, D. Paul and Judy. My love of art and travel, as well as my sense of determination comes directly from them, and I love them deeply for it.

And I'd be nowhere without my ARC team and delightful beta readers, especially Ian Morris and Ian Murphy.

ABOUT THE AUTHOR

Christy Nicholas writes under several pen names, including Rowan Dillon, CN Jackson, and Emeline Rhys. She's an author, artist, and accountant. After she failed to become an airline pilot, she quit her ceaseless pursuit of careers that began with the letter "A" and decided to concentrate on her writing. Since she has Project Completion Compulsion, she is one of the few authors with no unfinished novels.

Christy has her hands in many crafts, including digital art, beaded jewelry, writing, and photography. In real life, she's a CPA, but having grown up with art all around her (her mother, grandmother, and great-grandmother are/were all artists), it sort of infected her, as it were. She wants to expose the incredible beauty in this world, hidden beneath the everyday grime of familiarity and habit, and share it with others. She uses characters out of time and places infused with magic and myth, writing magical realism stories in both historical fantasy and time-travel flavors.

Social Media Links:
Blog: www.GreenDragonArtist.net
Website: www.GreenDragonArtist.com
Facebook: www.facebook.com/greendragonauthor
Instagram: www.instagram.com/greendragonartist9